# THE FUNDAMENTALS OF
# LISTING & SELLING
## COMMERCIAL REAL ESTATE

## LOREN K. KEIM

ISBN 0-7414-4369-4

Published by:

**INFI∞ITY**
PUBLISHING.COM
1094 New DeHaven Street, Suite 100
West Conshohocken, PA 19428-2713
Info@buybooksontheweb.com
www.buybooksontheweb.com
Toll-free (877) BUY BOOK
Local Phone (610) 941-9999
Fax (610) 941-9959

*Printed in the United States of America*

*Printed on Recycled Paper*

*Published November 2007*

# Table of Contents

# Introduction

One of my mentors, Ralph Williams, once told me that Commercial Real Estate is the tip of the iceberg of free society.  Without the ability to buy, sell and trade real property, we don't truly own anything and we really can't be a free capitalistic society.

The Commercial Real Estate Industry touches virtually every aspect of business in the United States and most of the free world.  Very few companies can grow without acquiring more land or additional office space, patients can't use the services of a hospital unless it's constructed and consumers can't shop at a Wal-Mart without the development of Real Property.

Commercial Real Estate encompasses all aspects of sales, leasing, management, investment in or improvement of retail property, investment property, farmland, businesses, industries, medical facilities and dozens of other types of property.  Our job in the industry is to assist in the lease, management or sales of property, and to advise our clients of their best courses of action when deciding how to invest in or improve real property or a commercial asset.

We work directly with industry leaders, community leaders, government officials, lawyers, zoning officers, accountants, mortgage companies, banks, title companies, appraisers, utility companies and everyone in between to put together sales or develop property to its full potential for a client.  While we can't make decisions for our clients, we can assist them in making better informed decisions, and we can help our clients to understand what the highest and best use may be for a particular property, or what type of investment vehicle might be best for our client.

We work with property owners who may want to sell a property, lease a property, have a property managed or determine what use might be better for the property than the current use.  We work with users of properties to find the best location for their business or investment, to determine if it's better for the user to lease a property or purchase and to understand the tax implications of their decisions. Additionally, we work with investors to determine which real estate venture might be their best investment to meet their particular goals and needs.

Commercial real estate agents and brokers work with individuals, investors, organizations and corporations to develop property to its highest potential. Our careers include many specializations. Some commercial associates specialize in particular types of property, such as office property, developable farmland or even amusement parks. Other commercial associates specialize in particular forms of consulting work for Real Estate Investment Trusts, insurance companies or utility companies. Still others work in specialized areas such as resort management or assist government agencies with redevelopment of industrial sites or reclamation of land.

The path you choose to take now, venturing into a career in commercial real estate, may open many unexpected doors in the future.

Your responsibilities as a commercial realtor or broker include:

**For Sellers or Property Owners:**

- **Hold or Sell Analysis** – Analyze the market to determine what course of action is best for a property owner. Is it better to hold onto the property longer, or would an owner be better suited selling the commercial property? This analysis may include projections of cash flows, and determination of internal rate of return.

- **Property Management** – Assist the owner by leasing and / or managing the day to day situations that arise in any real estate investment. Management may include suggestions of how to create more value in the property.

3 story multi-tenant Office Building with central common atrium.

- **Property Leasing** – Finding tenants for a property owner's commercial real estate. This may include advice on creating a niche for the property, or ways to attract more solid long term tenants.

8

- **Property Sale or Marketing** – Determining the best course of action in order to maximize the sales price on a property and find the best possible buyer.

## For Buyers, Tenants or Investors:

- **Investment Analysis** – Provide an investor or buyer with comparisons of various properties or types of property and their cash flows or investment returns in order to determine what situation may be best for the investor or buyer.

- **Site Selection** – Assist the investor or buyer with locating a site that meets the client's needs. Assist with demographic data to support the client's business or investment goals. An agent may also be required to assist with determining the site's suitability based on zoning regulations, environmental conditions and financing considerations.

- **Cash Flow Analysis / Return on Investment** – What kind of return can an investor expect on a particular real estate investment? Agents provide projections of potential future income and analysis of potential return on the property.

## For both Sellers / Owners and Buyers / Investors:

- **Property or Business Valuations** – Any property owner wants to know what their property is worth to a buyer and what the highest sales price or lease price is possible in the current market. Buyers or Investors want to know what a fair price may be for the same property or business, and will want to know what the best investment may be at this point in time.

- **Feasability Studies** – Conduct a market study with the help of Real Estate Appraisers and engineers to determine the highest and best use of a property, or forecast a project's likelihood of success.

- **Exchange Opportunities** – Tax-deferral benefits may make it worthwhile to exchange the property, or use a 1031 deferred exchange.

Commercial Real Estate is an exciting and rewarding field of study and can lead to dozens of different career opportunities. Whether someone is starting their first small business, or developing a parcel of land, or considering an investment in real estate rather than an investment in a mutual fund or money market, the understanding of commercial real estate is fundamental to their decisions.

This text is broken into two primary sections: the *Fundamentals of Commercial Real Estate* and the *Practice of Commercial Real Estate*. To begin your career, you'll need to understand exactly what you're selling, how it is priced, how it is financed and what legal documents must be used to convey the sale or lease. For that reason, our goal in the first section is to build a foundation for your career by introducing you to the key elements necessary to be successful in commercial real estate. We'll examine the diverse forms that commercial property takes, and the important terms used by those in the field to explain and understand a type of property. Next, we'll explore the different methods of determining value in the eyes of property users, investors, real estate professionals and appraisers. Then we'll consider how commercial real estate can be financed and how it may be leased. The section will conclude with an examination of the legal documents including listing contracts, sales agreements and lease contracts.

The second section of the text will introduce and explore the practical world of Commercial Real Estate. You'll be introduced to the difference between working with owners or sellers and buyers or tenants and what each wants from your relationship. This section will introduce how to find different sources of business to prospect, how to present yourself to those prospects and how to determine the value of the property. We'll explain methods for marketing commercial and investment real estate, and how to truly service your owners or sellers. The last chapters will explain how to work with buyers, investors and tenants to locate the perfect property and how to negotiate the purchase or lease. Finally, we'll go through an outline of where you can find additional information.

Again, I welcome you to the wonderful world of Commercial Real Estate. It's a big world, full of lots of legal and mathematical questions. It can be a very frustrating roller coaster ride of a career, but it can also be a very exciting, challenging and rewarding career. It's one of the few careers where your income truly is limited only by your imagination. Like any elephant, we suggest you eat it one small bite at a time, and enjoy the journey!

When you finish this text, please visit us at www.RealEstatesNextLevel.com

# Introduction to Commercial Property

## Types of Commercial Investment Real Estate

In an introductory text like this one, it would be impossible to itemize every single type of real estate investment vehicle. There are literally hundreds of real estate investments. Some are passive, like REITs (Real Estate Investment Trusts) and TICs (Tenants in Common) projects, and some are very hands-on, like buying an existing business or developing a mixed use parcel of land.

My goal is to provide you with a broad understanding of the various major commercial real estate investments. Many experts and organizations have tried to categorize commercial and investment real estate into between five and twelve different broad categories. I have divided active commercial and investment real estate into ten broad categories.

1. Office Buildings / Office Space
2. Retail Buildings / Retail Space
3. Shopping Centers
4. Industrial / Flexible Space
5. Hospitality Property
6. Multifamily Property
7. Farm and Ranch Property
8. Business Opportunity
9. Vacant Developable Land
10. Senior Housing / Long Term Care Facilities

Each of these categories will be developed in detail in the following pages.

# Office Buildings / Office Space

What are office buildings, really? What does Class A space mean? What's the difference between a low rise building and a high rise building?

An office building or office space is a place where people work, answer telephones, have coffee breaks and chat around the water cooler. An office building can be as simple as a home in a business district converted to be used for office purposes, or as complex as a fifty story office tower. Most recently constructed office buildings are simply large boxes of space, carved up by architects into various smaller boxes, containing rooms or collections of rooms, to fit the needs of the end user. These buildings can be occupied by a single end user, or can be broken up into multiple users or tenants.

Modern High Tech Office Facilities are wired with access to high speed computer lines

Office buildings are generally categorized three different ways. They are categorized by the quality of the space (Class A, Class B, Class C), by the height of the building (low rise, mid rise or high rise) or by usable space or square footage.

## A, B or C Classification

Despite many attempts by organizations to classify quality of space, there is no hard and fast definition. I realize that there are probably several lifelong commercial brokers now running to their computers to write me nasty notes explaining that there are definitive determining factors for Class A versus Class C. However, the determination of Classes of Office Space continues to be subjective in our various marketplaces. Despite dozens of articles and definitions, experts can not completely agree on any one definition, and commercial real estate brokers in their respective marketplaces do not follow any one set of definitions. The basic rules of thumb are as follows:

<u>Class A</u> generally means that the property is high quality and is either new or in new condition. The space should have a modern design, the finish work should be excellent, and the ability for high speed communications must be in place. Some brokers additionally determine Class A by location. For example, an excellent location by the cross roads of two interstates might earn a designation of Class A, while a similar

building downtown next to a brown-field might be considered Class B. Class A properties tend to command the highest rental rates in a market.

**Class B** offices are generally in good condition, and highly rentable. They tend to command a lower rental rate than Class A properties, and may not have all the bells and whistles of Class A property in the same area.

**Class C** office properties generally are "dated" or have some functional obsolescence, such as poor layouts or lack of high speed computer line availability. These properties may be found in less desirable locations.

Okay, let me be perfectly honest for a minute. You will probably never see an advertisement reading "Spectacular Class C Office Space available for just $XX per square foot!" Who actually determines the "Class" of each property being marketed? The Real Estate Broker or associate that is listing the property for lease or sale is the one who sets the label in their advertising and online.

Real Estate brokers and associates will typically try to slant upward the value of the property they are marketing. So what is an honest comparison between true Class A office space and Class B office space?

As stated above, the differences between the classes have to do primarily with condition and amenities, although location can often play a key role as well. These classifications can be somewhat subjective because these terms "A" and "B" are not set in stone. Brand new space is typically considered Class A when it is built.

Can Class B space be updated to Class A? Location can't be changed, so if the building is located in a downtown area in a secondary market, it may be difficult to market as Class A. However, replacing windows, replacing carpeting, updating the lobby to add a waterfall or garden, and configuring the layout to fit most modern office work can bring a property back up to the Class A level.

## Types of Office Buildings

There are 3 types of office building: Low Rise, Mid Rise and High Rise.

- Low Rise is considered to be any office building that is less than 7 stories.
- Mid Rise is any office building between 7 and 25 stories.
- High Rise is anything above 25 stories.

High Rise Office Building

## Classifications of Office Properties

- **Office Building** – Any building primarily used for business functions.
- **Medical Office Building** – Office buildings containing space designated specifically for medical functions including medical labs, physician's offices, dental offices and other medical functions.
- **R&D Office Building** – Office buildings that contain space used for research and development activities. These types of buildings may include specific lab space and storage areas.
- **Institutional / Governmental** – Offices used specifically for government agencies and purposes.
- **Executive Office Suites** – A "Business Center" that provides the tenants with space for their business and shared space that may be used for conference rooms, receptionists and mail service that are common between different businesses.
- **Office Condos** – A portion of an office building that can be deeded and occupied by an individual or business.

## Measuring Office Space

When selling an office building for a single user, a Realtor can often find the square footage or size of the building by consulting the original building plans, or information kept by the local tax records. If you, as a Realtor, are going to represent space in an office building for lease, you'll need to consider what space is actually being leased. Office buildings generally have <u>Usable Space</u> or <u>Rentable Space</u> and <u>Common Areas</u>. Common Areas are those areas that are shared by multiple tenants including common bathrooms, hallways, elevators, mechanical rooms and lobbies.

A complete set of standards for measuring Rentable Space have been created by the Building Owners and Managers Association (BOMA). Understanding the BOMA standards takes a fair bit of study and practice. Our purpose in this course is to give you a broad understanding the Commercial Real Estate Industry, and the BOMA standards encompass 18 double sided pages plus a set of 26 commonly asked questions, so we won't go into the entire code here. To obtain a complete set of these standards, you can call BOMA at 1-800-426-6292 or order them online at www.boma.org. Local chapters of BOMA also offer half day classes on how to apply the standards.

In some specific areas, like New York City and Washington, D.C., local real estate organizations have come up with alternative plans for measuring space. The Real Estate Board of New York has created the **REBNY Standard**, which is used to measure leased office space in the New York metropolitan area, including nearby parts of Connecticut and New Jersey. The **GWCAR Standard** is used to measure leased office space in the Washington, D.C. metropolitan area, including nearby parts of Maryland and Virginia.

# Common Areas

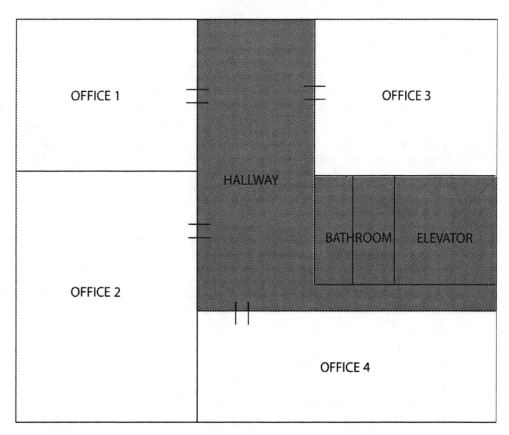

**Shaded areas represent common space including elevators, staircases, common bathrooms and hallways.**

There are two more simple methods used by many commercial realtors to measure space. Please keep in mind that the preferred method of measurement is the BOMA system. Many realtors simply measure the exterior dimensions of the building and reduce it by any common areas such as common bathrooms or lobbies. Other agents determine the space of the property by obtaining an architect's drawing or building plan and multiplying the dimensions. If a plan of the building is unavailable, a Realtor may be forced to measure the space by hand. I always suggest drawing the space as you measure in order to make sure you include the entire space. Hallways, closets and bathrooms within a tenant's private area are all part of the space the tenant is leasing.

**Usable Space** or **Rentable Space** is that space used exclusively by the tenant. That may include staircases if the tenant leases multiple floors. Tenants in this type of commercial space, as well as tenants in retail or industrial, typically pay for office space on a per square foot basis. A commercial realtor should be very adept at measuring this space. If you're representing a property owner, the owner will want an accurate determination of size so they don't lose potential income. Prospective tenants will want an accurate determination so they don't overpay for the space they are leasing.

# Retail Buildings / Retail Space

In this text, we're defining Retail space as a separate class from Shopping Centers. Shopping Centers are groups of retail spaces combined in a single center and managed as a single center. Retail space is often categorized either by the type of building that is housing the space, such as a corner free standing building versus a big box store, or differentiated by the type of retail usage, such as automotive or prepared food.

For example, if you have a prospective buyer or tenant looking to open a restaurant, it helps to have a property already configured for a restaurant. A tavern will need a liquor license, and an automotive service station will need bays to hold cars and proper zoning for automotive use.

The various types of retail can be limited only by your imagination, but the major categories are defined below.

## Major Types of Retail Building

- **Free Standing** – This can refer to anything from a McDonald to a CVS or an independent tavern. A free standing or detached commercial property that is independent from other buildings around it.

- **Pad Site** - Similar to a Free Standing Building, a Pad Site is a single user detached property. However, a pad site is an out parcel of a larger center. Typical pad sites are occupied by fast food, gas stations, or banks.
- **Shopping Center** – We'll be covering this type in the next section.
- **Big Box Retail** – Any retail that requires large amounts of space, such as pharmacies, grocery stores, department stores, large hardware stores, computer stores, video and appliance stores. Typically these stores can be reconfigured with temporary walls.
- **Small Box Retail** – Any retail that requires little more than 4 walls and decorating. Stores include clothing stores, antique shops, gift shops, small appliance stores.
- **Special Use** – An automotive repair garage is set up as a specific use that lends itself best to an automotive type use, without significant conversion. A commercial greenhouse is another example of a special use property.
- **Retail Condo** – Big Box or Small Box retail generally refers to either a free standing building or a space that can be leased in a shopping center or strip mall. Some retail buildings have been converted to Condominiums so that the user or an investor can purchase a piece of a larger building.
- **Residential Conversion** – Often found in older sections of cities and towns, residential properties that have been converted into neighborhood taverns, small restaurants, and gift shops.

## Major Types of Retail Uses:

We certainly can't cover every type of retail use in this text, but we can highlight some of the most common retail properties:

- **Auto Related** - Any property or building used as a repair or service garage, gas station, parking garage or any other auto related use.
- **Auto and Truck Sales** - This category includes both new and used auto and truck dealerships.
- **Prepared Food Related** – A restaurant, fast food service, cafeteria, ice cream / dessert service, coffee house and any other food serving property.

Melt Restaurant in the Promonade Shops at Saucon Valley in Eastern Pennsylvania

- **Taverns and Drinking Related** - Businesses engaged in the retail sales of alcoholic drinks, such as beer, wine, and liquor, for consumption on the premises. Prepared foods may or may not also be served in taverns or drinking establishments.
- **Grocery Stores** – Retail sales of food items for home consumption.
- **Convenience Stores** – Sales of convenience items including some groceries. These stores are often paired with a gas station.
- **Specialty Food Stores** – Retail sales of specialty food for home consumption, including meat, fish, fruits and vegetables, candy and nuts, dairy products, retail bakeries, health foods, and ethnic foods.
- **Daycare / Nursery** – A facility to provide supervision, recreation, and possibly schooling or training of children. This category also includes Adult and Senior Daycare centers.
- **Building Materials and Supplies**- Retail establishments that sell lumber or building materials to the public. Although many building supply stores also sell wholesale to contractors, they are still considered to be retail. These stores include paint, glass, and wallpaper stores.
- **Hardware Stores** – A retail outlet that sells tools, builder's hardware, locks, security hardware, and a minimum of building materials.
- **Furniture Stores** – Retails that is primarily engaged in selling new household furniture, including beds and mattresses. This category could include specialty furniture such as baby furniture, sleep furniture, and the like.
- **Appliance Stores** - Retail sale of major appliances including refrigerators, ranges or stoves, home freezers, washers, dryers and other household appliances.
- **Consumer Electronics Stores** - Retail sale of audio, video and computer equipment including computers, televisions and video equipment, stereo equipment, sound reproducing equipment, and other consumer electronics equipment. Stores may also sell computer peripheral equipment, software, movies, and music.
- **Camera and Photographic Equipment** – This category can be included in Consumer Electronic Stores or can be a specialty store just concerned with photography.
- **Lawn / Garden Shops** – Sales of plants, trees, shrubs, landscaping supplies, soil, fertilizers and garden equipment.
- **Apparel, Shoe, Accessory Stores** – Retailers engaged in selling clothing, shoes or accessories.
- **Department, Variety and General Merchandise Stores** - Stores that offer diverse product lines such as apparel, dry goods, furniture, home furnishings, appliances, video equipment and hardware.
- **Pharmacies / Drug Stores** – Sales of prescription drugs, cosmetics, toiletries and similar items.

- **Liquor Stores** – Retail sales of packaged alcoholic beverages for home consumption.
- **Antique Stores** – Antique merchandise such as furniture, nick-nacks, clothing, shoes and books.
- **Book Stores** – Retail sales of new books and periodicals, and re-sales of some books.
- **Sporting Goods** – Sales of equipment for sports (such as football, basketball, hockey, etc) as well as sales of exercise equipment (such as bicycles, weight lifting equipment, etc), and outdoor equipment (such as hunting, camping, fishing, skiing, etc).
- **Office Supplies** – Retail sales of office supplies, stamp, stationary, toner, computer media and similar supplies.
- **Jewelry** – Retail sales of diamonds, precious stones, rings, bracelets, watches, clocks and fine silverware.
- **Hobby Shop / Toys / Game Shops** – Retail sales of toys, games, hobbies, and craft kits or supplies.
- **Gift / Souvenir and Novelty Stores** – Retail sales of gifts and novelty merchandise, greeting cards, collectibles and party supplies.
- **Florists** – Retail sales of flowers and growing plants. Category also includes gift baskets.
- **Miscellaneous** – Any retail store that doesn't fit another category!

# Shopping Centers

Shopping Centers exist in every part of the United States and around the world. They can be found in many different configurations. The International Council of Shopping Centers (ICSC) has defined a Shopping Center to be "*a group of retail and other commercial establishments that is planned, developed, owned and managed as a single property. On-site parking is provided. The center's size and orientation are generally determined by the market characteristics of the trade area served by the center.*"[1]

A Shopping Center generally takes one of two forms. The first is an "Open Air Center", which simply refers to a shopping center or complex that is not enclosed. Open Air Centers may have canopies connecting storefronts, and almost always have walkways in front of or between the storefronts, but the store fronts are not enclosed. Some Open Air Centers are simple strip centers with a straight row of attached retail or commercial stores. Some are U-shaped with a large anchor store in the center, or L-shaped with a large anchor store at either end.

[1] International Council of Shopping Centers Definitions

The second most prevalent form of Shopping Center is the Mall. This form of Shopping Center has an enclosed walkway. Storefronts are often turned inside, away from the parking areas, to face the interior enclosed space.

Although two primary forms exist for Shopping Centers, there are many centers that exhibit the characteristics of both. Some have stores facing inside, with an enclosed mall area or walkway, and have additional stores facing out in the Open Air fashion. These centers are hybrid forms.

The International Council of Shopping Centers (ICSC) has defined eight major types of shopping center. These various types are classified primarily by their size and their types of goods and services sold. You will find that even with these broad classifications, hybrids of various types exist and new types have been developed each decade.

## Types of Shopping Centers[2]:

### Mall Forms

- **Regional Center**: This form of mall contains large anchor tenants, such as a traditional department store (Macys, JC Penney), an upscale department store (Neiman Marcus, Saks Fifth Avenue), discount department store (Walmart, Target), or fashion department store and many specialty stores and stores of general merchandise such as apparel and services. These centers are generally enclosed with stores facing a center walkway or atrium. A Regional Center is considered by the ICSC to be 400,000 to 800,000 square feet and draws most customers from a 5 to 15 mile radius.

- **Super regional Center**: The primary difference between Regional and Super Regional Centers is size. Considered by the ICSC to be over 800,000 square feet, this form of mall has more anchor tenants and a larger mix of specialty stores and merchandise. Frequently, these malls are multi story configurations. Super Regional Centers draw their primary customers from a 25 mile radius

### Open Air Forms

- **Neighborhood Center**: The local neighborhood center pulls most of their clients from within 3 miles of the center. Generally configured as a straight-line strip center and parking located directly in the front. These centers may have a canopy or other façade to provide shade and protection from inclement weather, or to tie the center together. The tenants tend to be stores catering to the daily needs of the

---

[2] Provided by the International Council of Shopping Centers.

local community.  According to ICSC's SCORE publication, approximately half of these centers are anchored by a supermarket, while about a third are anchored by a drugstore. Typical stores found in neighborhood centers include those drugs, sundries, snacks and personal services.

- **Community Center**: A community center draws up to 6 miles from the center and typically offers a wider range of products than the neighborhood center. Community centers often offer apparel and services.  Common anchor tenants for community centers are supermarkets, large drugstores, and discount department stores.  Community center tenants can sometimes include big-box category-dominant retailers such as Home Depot, Lowes, Best Buy, Toys R Us, TJ Max or other big box retailers.  The center may be configured in a straight line strip, or may be laid out in an L or U shape, depending on the site and design. Community shopping centers include a wide variety of designs. Community centers can be themed or targeted at particular groups.  For example, certain centers that are anchored by a large discount department store may have a majority focus of discount stores as tenants.

- **Power Center**: A power center is composed of several large anchors and very few smaller tenants.   The anchors may include discount department stores, off-price stores, warehouse clubs, or big box "category killers".

- **Lifestyle Center**: An open air center that is designed, in many cases, to resemble a historic downtown, or to be laid out for shoppers to browse and relax with exterior benches, fountains and eye pleasing designs.  This design is called "village clustered".  The key word for a Lifestyle Center is ambiance.  Generally located very close to affluent residential neighborhoods, Lifestyle Centers cater to the retail needs and "lifestyle" pursuits of consumers in its trading area.  They are designed

A Lifestyle Center known as the Promenade Shops at Saucon Valley creates the atmosphere of a downtown, complete with center square, and fountain.

as much a place for residents to stop, browse, and have a casual cup or coffee or lunch as they are for shopping.  Typical tenants are upscale national chain specialty stores, high end restaurants and entertainment. These centers may be anchored by one or more conventional or fashion specialty department stores.

Because a common theme of Lifestyle Centers is a downtown look, there are often streets between stores, and parking is located throughout the exterior of the center.

- **Theme / Festival Center**: Often located in urban areas, these centers may be an adaptive re-use of older buildings or a historic district. Theme centers may be included as part of mixed-use projects in redevelopment areas. Theme or Festival Centers generally have a unifying theme that is carried out by the individual shops and often their merchandise. This unifying theme may be found in the center's architectural design. A common element of these centers is entertainment, although some rely solely on the shopping experience. Although Theme Centers are generally targeted at tourists, they may also attract local customers. Theme or festival centers may be anchored by restaurants and entertainment facilities.

- **Outlet Center**: Outlet Centers draw from a wide radius of 25 to 75 miles. Shoppers look for discounts on brand name products. Typically, these centers include manufacturers' and retailers' outlet stores selling brand-name goods at a discount. Although outlet centers are often unanchored, certain brand-name stores may serve to attract customers and other tenants to the center. Layouts of outlet centers may be consistent with open air strip centers, or may be village clustered, like Lifestyle Centers. There are also some enclosed outlet centers throughout North America.

# Industrial / Flexible Space

Industrial property is often described as either "light industrial" or "heavy industrial". Although the difference between light and heavy industrial is often vague, Light Industrial typically refers to lower impact storage and manufacturing. Light Industrial uses may include warehousing, wholesaling, assembly of products or research and development.

Heavy Industrial properties can have a very specific use, such as the steel smelting towers pictured above.

Heavy industrial typically refers to manufacturing, producing, processing or refining of products or raw materials. Additionally, Heavy industrial often requires larger land parcels and accessibility to transportation such as rail lines or major highways.

Information on industrial development and calculations of the benefits of industrial development can be found through the National Association of Industrial and Office Properties at www.NAIOP.org.

## Types of Industrial Property

Industrial property can be categorized dozens of different ways depending on the type of property, the use, or the construction. The basic forms of industrial property are:

- **<u>Flexible or Flex Space</u>** – large bulk buildings that can be broken into smaller units. Often Flex Space can be finished into warehouse, light manufacturing or office space. Many flexible buildings have a front entrance at ground level for offices, and a rear entrance at truck level or dock height.

- **<u>Distribution / Warehouse</u>** – Also known as bulk properties, distribution warehouses are generally walls, a roof and flooring. They tend to be large buildings and are used for storage and distribution of materials, products or equipment. Some distribution warehouses are measured in cubic feet because height can be important to some types of storage and distribution. A distribution warehouse will generally have several to many loading docks at truck level or docking height, or may be set up with drive-in doors for trucks. These buildings generally have less than 15% office space.

- **<u>Manufacturing</u>** – Manufacturing can be either a heavy industrial or a light industrial use depending on the product and the process to create the product. Manufacturing property can be a single building or a collection of buildings. Some products are even manufactured or assembled outside. Manufacturing buildings or facilities include production, refinement, and assembly.

- **<u>Research and Development</u>** – R&D can fall under either office space or industrial space depending on the type of research and development. R&D uses that require use of heavy equipment may require an industrial property. Additionally, users may require laboratories, "clean rooms" for chip manufacturing or chemical processes or analysis.

- **<u>Self Storage / Mini Warehouse</u>** – Commercial facilities that allow individuals or companies to rent space smaller than a warehouse for storage of equipment, products, goods or personal items. Self Storage facilities and Mini Warehouse facilities are often located in light industrial zones.

- **Truck Terminal** – Facilities where goods or products are transferred between trucks or between trucks and railroads. Buildings can be used for short term storage.

- **Cold Storage / Refrigerated Space** – A specific type of warehouse / distribution space that requires refrigeration. These properties are often measured in cubic feet because ceiling height is important to the value of the storage space.

## Locations of Industrial Space

- **Business Park Industrial / Industrial Park** – Modern industrial property is carefully planned by developers and municipalities, and is often built close to highways and rail access. Parks for industrial use are created to keep much of these uses in close proximity to each other. Parks can share the cost of bringing in large utilities and technology, like gas lines or high speed internet lines, by sharing the cost among several end users. Many business parks are a mix of light industrial, office, warehousing and distribution uses.

- **Brownfields** – Central areas in major cities were used for heavy manufacturing at one time in our country's history. Factories were built close to the labor pool, and housing grew around the factories. In modern day America, many of these properties are located in areas that are difficult to access from the major highway systems. Redevelopment of these "brownfield" sites has been a major political goal for the last several decades.

The Bethlehem Steel site in Bethlehem Pennsylvania, at approximately 5 miles long, is currently the largest Brownfield project in the country. The site is being redeveloped into a business park and a waterfront casino.

- **Free Standing**- Sites that are developed for a single user are generally called Free Standing sites.

# Hospitality Properties

Hospitality properties are those properties concerned with lodging, vacations and recreation. This category of commercial real estate includes hotels, motels, bed & breakfasts, casinos, convention centers, golf courses, recreational cabins, spas and vacation rentals. The category may also include amusement parks, indoor water parks and similar uses.

Although some hospitality properties, like B&B's or recreational cabins tend to be updated infrequently, many hospitality properties can be very capital intensive, with continual updates, additions and remodeling. According to the International Society of Hospitality Consultants, real estate agents and brokers that specialize in this particular category or subcategory need to go beyond the typical analysis of buying and selling the property to identify value-added strategies, including remodeling and expansion, and repositioning strategies into their projections. Evaluations of particular properties or projects need to take into consideration industry trends, vacation and meeting trends, and capital markets.

## Categories of Hospitality Property

- Hotel / Motel
  - Economy / Limited Service
  - Full Service
  - Extended Stay Hotels
  - Resort / Convention Center
  - Bed and Breakfast / Country Inn
- Casino
- Luxury Spa
- Timeshare Complex / Shared Ownership
- Golf Course
- Marina
- Camp Ground / Recreational Cabins
- Amusement Park / Water Park / Indoor Water Park
- Special purpose (ski lodge, private beach, etc)
- Mixed Use / Combined Use Property

## Important Terms for Hospitality Property

- **RevPAR** - RevPAR stands for Revenue Per Available Room. This term is the industry standard for measuring the revenue-generation of any hotel property. It is calculated by multiplying the Average Daily Room Rate by the Occupancy Rate in order to give a single answer for the combination of revenue or price and occupancy or volume.

- **ADR** – stands for Average Daily Room Rate and is calculated by dividing the Gross Revenue from the rental of rooms by the number of occupied rooms during a specific period of time. This calculation shows the average room rate or price of a room for that period.

- **Occupancy Rate** – The number of hotel rooms leased or sold each night divided by the total number of rooms in the hotel or resort. This number is used to measure the average occupancy of the property.

## Types of Hotels

According to one industry estimate, there are approximately 62,000 establishments that provide overnight accommodations. This diverse industry includes everything from country inns and road side motels to luxury resorts, casino hotels and extended stay hotels. The industry covers a wide range of establishments varying greatly by size and by the amenities and services each offers their patrons. In order to work in this area of commercial real estate, whether doing sales of existing facilities or development of new facilities, you'll need to understand the industry and the value of each type of establishment.

- **Economy or Limited Service Hotel**- Often referred to as Motels, these generally provide limited amenities. A guest simply pays for a room for the night or for a period of time.

- **Full Service Hotel** – In addition to providing overnight accommodations, full service hotels typically offer additional amenities and additional services, which may generate additional revenue streams for the hotel owner. Amenities may include a swimming pool and fitness or exercise rooms. Services may include restaurants, a lounge, newsstand or banquet facilities that may be used to provide the owner with additional revenue.

- **Resort or Convention Center**- A resort is a self contained place to stay and to be entertained, offering recreational facilities and generally some business facilities as well. A typical resort includes restaurants, pools, a salon, some shopping and other forms of entertainment. Resorts can include golf courses, ski facilities, health spas, entertainment or shows, and even planned social activities for their guests. Typical resorts also offer convention or conference facilities in order to bring in more guests, and to combine business with pleasure.

Marriot World Center Convention Center in Lake Buena Vista, Florida.

- **Extended Stay Hotels** – Targeting the corporate business traveler and moving families, Extended Stay Hotels are designed to attract guests who stay longer periods of time, from 5 to 90 days. Rooms in these types of establishments often include kitchens, entertainment systems, desks or office space with access to the Internet. Amenities may include pools and fitness centers.

- **Bed & Breakfast or Country Inn** – Bed and Breakfasts are typically large single family homes that have been converted to rooms for rent. In a typical B&B, guests are given a bedroom in the home, and provided with a breakfast in the morning. Bathrooms may be private, or may be shared with other bedrooms. Bed and Breakfasts are often historic homes or homes in scenic or resort locations.


## Grading Hotels

Hotels are often ranked in a similar fashion to office buildings. While office buildings are often divided into Class A, Class B and Class C, Hotels may be ranked as Tier 1 through Tier 4. The tiers are based partly on the condition and location of the property, but are also based on the return and risk of the property.

o **Tier One** - Four and Five Star Hotels are generally considered to be Tier 1 or First Tier properties. Most Tier 1 or First Tear properties are located in popular resort areas or major metropolitan locations. They are generally newer quality hotels, or refurbished upscale hotels with lots of services and amenities. Some brokers believe that an excellent Three Star hotel in a very good location can also be a Tier 1 hotel.

o   **Tier Two**- Recently built hotels, within the last ten to fifteen years, in good locations.  Second Tier hotels typically need little or no updating, and generally compete on price rather than amenities.

o   **Tier Three** – Older hotels in good locations.  These hotels can often be updated or renovated to increase their market appeal.

o   **Tier Four** – Older hotels in fair or poor locations.

## Timeshares and Vacation Ownership

Timeshares and timeshare management have been included in some definitions of Hospitality Real Estate, but my belief is that timeshares tend to fall under a residential real estate use or even under multifamily housing.   However, commercial developers will look at a property to obtain its highest and best use.  In order to net the highest return for an investor, the best use of a particular property in a destination location may be to convert the property to a timeshare rather than a hotel or multifamily property.  When purchasing an apartment complex or mixed use property, as a real estate professional, you should carefully consider the possibility of conversion of the property into another use, such as condominiums or timeshares.

Timeshares are a fractional interest in a piece of property. This fractional interest generally takes the form of a certain amount of time an owner is purchasing for the use of the real estate.   There are four primary forms of shared ownership business models:

Marriot Vacation Club in Orlando, Florida.

•   **Timeshares / Vacation Ownership** – Sometimes considered to be a pre-paid vacation, timeshares or vacation ownership are typically the purchase of the use of an apartment or villa style accommodations in a managed resort environment.  Timeshares are typically broken down into "weeks".  The rights to use the apartment or villa can be fixed to a certain time period each year or every other year, or it can be floating, in which case the owner is able to use the apartment or villa each year for the period of time purchased, but the period can be shifted from year to year, as long as availability exists. Some floating units are limited to certain seasons or a specific range of weeks. These rights to use the property can be purchased for a specific period of time, like 20-50 years, or they can be an unlimited deeded use of the property. After development and sale of the project, it can be managed by the developer of the resort or by a management company. Typically, a buyer pays an upfront fee to purchase their timeshare, and then pays an ongoing annual maintenance fee, which often includes part of the property taxes, expenses and the management of the property. Vacation Ownership packages include Disney Vacation Club, Marriot Vacation Club and many others.

- **Fractional Ownership / Private Residence Clubs** – Like a timeshare or vacation ownership, a Fractional Properties or Private Residence Club allow a purchaser to buy a specific period of time or usage of a real estate investment. The difference is that Private Residence Clubs tend to be longer periods of ownership, from one month to three months, and tend to be a very high quality property, often with more services than the typical timeshare. Fractional ownership properties can be luxury apartments, condominiums or even detached single homes. Many of them are found in resort hotel environments. Examples of these types of ownership include the Ritz-Carlton Club and Marriot Grand Residence Club.

- **Destination Clubs** – The third type of vacation ownership is similar to both the timeshare concept and to private residence clubs, but a Destination Club allows a buyer to purchase membership in the club that owns several or many destinations, rather than buying the use rights of a specific property or complex in a particular location. For example, the club may purchase a group of properties in the Las Vegas, Orlando, New York, Paris and a few beach and mountain properties. A buyer into the club would have access to use any of these properties in proportion to their ownership interest in the club. Like a timeshare, the buyer will have ongoing maintenance fees.

- **Condo Hotels / Buy-To-Use-And-Let Offerings** – The relatively new concept of the condo hotel is a hybrid of condominiums and of timeshares or even rental units. A buyer or investor can purchase a specific unit in fee simple title. Although a buyer can use the unit as a principal residence, in most cases the buyer will make use of the property for their own personal use for only a small period of time each year, possibly from 2 to 6 weeks. The remainder of the time, the unit is managed by the hospitality operator in a rental program. The income derived from the rental of the unit is generally split between the operator and the owner. Developers for Condo Hotels include Pierre & Vacances, Sol Melia and Intrawest.

- **Mixed Use** – In many destination locations around the world, developments have been successfully implemented where a mix of different hospitality business models are integrated within the same resort environment. These can include:

  o Traditional hotel rooms and suites
  o Vacation Ownership / Timeshares
  o Fractional Ownership
  o Buy-to-Use-and-Let Ownership
  o Serviced Whole Ownership

Management of timeshares can be either a commercial venture or a residential management venture. Often timeshares are tied in with other hospitality real estate, such as an amusement park, ski lodge or casino.

# Multi-Family Property

Multi-family housing can simply be defined as any building with more than one residential unit. Any apartment building or apartment complex falls into the category of multifamily Housing. Realtors and mortgage companies separate multifamily housing into two primary groups. Anything that is between one and four units is considered to be residential in the eyes of a mortgage lender. Any building or complex that is five units or above is considered to be a commercial property, and the rules for lending are different.

Investors seek to purchase or develop multifamily housing complexes in order to create an income stream that provides them with a high return on their investment. Commercial real estate investors often begin investing in real estate by purchasing multifamily housing. These buyers can often grow to purchase larger and larger properties.

As a real estate agent or consultant, your job may be to assist a property seller with determining the best asking price, or assist a potential buyer or investor with analyzing and buying a property, or developing a property for multi-family use.

Sources for information about multifamily housing include the National Apartment Association (www.NAAHQ.org), the Institute of Real Estate Management (www.IREM.org), and the National Multi Housing Council (www.NMHC.org).

## Categories of Multi-Family Dwellings:

Multifamily housing can be categorized in several different ways. Many experts categorize properties by the condition, age and quality of construction, classifying each property "AA" through "D". Other industry experts categorize the various types of multifamily housing by both density and height, although various organizations from appraisers to architects to property management companies to construction firms have developed very different uses for the same classification terms, such as Mid-Rise and High-Rise.

The list of categories below includes some classifications specific to the height of the property, the age of the property, or the ownership form, such as co-operatives and condominiums.

- **Conversion**- Residential or dwellings or commercial properties converted into multiple family dwellings.

- **Duplex or Triplex** - Although the actual definition of a duplex is an apartment that spans 2 floors, the term is generally

The former Johnson Machine Building along the Lehigh River in Bethlehem, Pennsylvania is an example of a conversion and adaptive reuse project. The old plant has been converted into luxury waterfront condos with a health club, coffee shop and restaurant.

used by real estate professionals to refer to a building that was built specifically as a 2 unit. A triplex refers to a building built as a 3 unit.

- **Garden Apartments** – Generally refers to a low-rise, one to three story, building or group of buildings that have communal lawn area or gardens. Garden apartments are generally suburban apartments.

- **Mid Rise** – The term is defined differently by appraisers, architects, lenders, property management groups and other organizations. Some appraisers define mid rise as four to six stories, some five to eight stories, and others between fifty and one hundred fifty feet in height. One dictionary even defines a mid rise building as "moderately tall". Some organizations go so far as to claim that a building must contain a certain density of apartment in order to be considered a Mid Rise. Our rule of thumb is four to nine stories.

- **High Rise** – As with Mid Rise definitions, High Rise definitions are equally as difficult to pin down. Some claim a High Rise is anything over six stories, some claim it's over eight, ten or twelve stories and still others claim it is any multifamily building exceeding 120 or 150 feet. Our answer is ten stories or greater.

- **<u>Mobile Home Park</u>** – A suburban property with mobile homes. The park may share one source of water or sewage and in many cases the tenant provides their own mobile home and simply rents the lot from the park owner.

- **<u>Condominiums</u>** – A multifamily housing project that has been developed to allow individual owners to take title to a specific unit in the building or complex. The owner purchases the interior of the unit, and shares the common areas, such as a lobby, yard or amenities, with other owners in the building or complex. An owner must pay a monthly or annual fee for their share of the maintenance and management of the property.

- **<u>Cooperatives</u>** – A complex or building that is owned by an association or group of people. All of the owners own a share of the total building or complex, and are assigned a unit for their use. Unlike a condominium, the owner does not specifically own the interior of their unit.

- **<u>Mixed Use</u>** – Any combination of residential and commercial use.

## Methods of comparison for Multifamily Property

As a real estate professional, buyers and sellers will ask you to evaluate multifamily housing. There are two primary types of comparison when evaluating investment property in general and multifamily property in particular. The first form of evaluation is to compare the property with other similar properties in the same geographic area. Different investors prefer different comparison techniques. Some make property comparisons based on a simple price per unit formula. Others compare properties based on the GIM or Gross Income Multiplier and still others use the property's Cap Rate, based on the net operating income of the property. Each of these methods is a straight comparison with competing or recently sold properties in the same area.

The second form of evaluation is used to compare a property or group of properties with other investments. Cash on Cash Return, Internal Rate of Return or Net Present Value calculations, which will be discussed in Chapter 3, evaluate the true economic gain of the property by factoring the long term income stream and ultimate appreciation of the property into the evaluation of the current value of the asset.

**Comparing properties by Price Per Unit** – (Sales Price / Number of Units) - A simple calculation of the sales price divided by the number of units in any particular property gives you the price per unit. This calculation should only be used when comparing buildings of similar age and similar units in the same area. It is meaningless, for example, to compare the average price per unit of multifamily dwellings in Houston when you're trying to determine a price range for a property in Denver. Many investors like this calculation because its relatively simple. However, the number does little to give us an indication of what type of return a particular property is generating. Each investor has their own way of determining if an investment is right for them, but investors should be most concerned about the return on their investment based on the risk they're taking. If the return on their investment is only 5%, for example, and they can buy US Government Bonds with a return of 6%, without the risk of buying real estate, and with more liquidity than real estate, then an investor should carefully consider their options.

**Comparing properties by Gross Income Multiplier (GIM)** – (Sales Price / Scheduled Gross Income) - As with price per unit, I am not a fan of using Gross Income Multipliers. This is again a simplistic way of comparing properties. The GIM is equal to the sales price divided by the scheduled gross income of the property. Some investors use a yearly gross income, and some use a monthly gross income. In either case, you must be consistent when comparing properties. The benefit of a GIM is that you don't have to research the expenses of the property. The risk of using a GIM for calculations is that one property's expenses may be significantly different than another. In one property, the owner may pay for the heat, or in another, a municipal authority may have much higher rates for water and sewer usage. Once again, I find it extremely important to truly know the bottom line – what is the return an investor will receive on his investment.

**Cap Rate** – (Net Operating Income / Sales Price) - Short for Capitalization Rate, the Cap Rate is a simple attempt to compare various properties based on their return. In simplest terms, the Net Operating Income is derived by taking the total of all rents per year (the Gross Income) and deducting any expenses the owner pays except the principal and interest of the mortgage. In other words, take the Gross Income and deduct the property taxes, property insurance, annual maintenance and any utility bills the owner pays each year. This number should also take vacancies into account. After determining the NOI, divide that number by the sales price and that will give you a quick return on investment.

Although this is a popular method used by investors and an easy calculation to compare properties, there are many shortcomings of this calculation. The rate of return derived from this calculation is not a true depiction of the income because it's a snapshot of one year's estimated net operating income. From an investment perspective, it does not take into account the type of loan the investor is able to obtain, the investor's tax structure and so on. From a comparison perspective, because it is a snapshot in time of one year, appreciation for the area is not considered in the calculation. An investment property in Allentown, Pennsylvania, for example, may have a Cap Rate of 9%, where a similar investment property in New York City may have a Cap Rate of 4.5%. A straight comparison of Cap Rates may lead an investor to believe the return in Allentown is better. However, the New York property may have such a high rate of appreciation for income or property value that the overall return for the New York property could be greater. That is why Cap Rate comparisons are generally only effective to compare various homes in the same geographic area.

**Cash on Cash Return** – (Net Profit / Cash Invested) - The cash-on-cash return rate is also known as the equity dividend rate, equity cap rate, and cash-throw-off rate. Cash on Cash Return is a far more complete determination of the return on a property. It takes into consideration the actual cash invested by the buyer, including the down payment and closing costs, and the mortgage payment in order to give a true picture of what kind of return an investor will receive on a particular property. Although we'll discuss this calculation in greater detail later in this text, the process is as follows:

Cash Invested = Down Payment + Closing Costs to purchase

Gross Income – Vacancies = Adjusted Gross Income or Effective Gross Income

Expenses = All expenses paid by the owner

Net Operating Income = Effective Gross Income – Expenses

Net Profit = NOI – Yearly Mortgage Payments (debt service)

Cash on Cash Return = Net Profit / Cash Invested

# Farm and Ranch Property

Over the years, I've had some pretty strong arguments from other real estate professionals as to whether or not farm properties qualify as commercial real estate. In many cases they can qualify as either commercial or residential, but there are specific reasons I'm including them in this text as a primary form of commercial property.

First, commercial farms growing wheat or corn, and commercial horse facilities such as those breeding and training thoroughbreds, or those deriving an income from boarding horses and training riders, do not

easily fit into any other form of commercial real estate. Many of these properties require commercial loans, and many are used as a primary business for the owners.

Secondly, large real estate investors and large commercial investors look to develop new commercial real estate projects. A project may be done as a "re-development" on the site of an existing or prior commercial or residential use. More often, however, these developments are done on farms or large land parcels. If you're assisting in site location and site development for a builder, developer or investment group, you need to be familiar with farms.

## Types of Commercial Farm Uses:

- <u>Commercial Boarding Facility</u> – Income is derived from boarding "tenant" horses and collecting a monthly fee for housing the horses, turning them out, feeding and caring for them. A secondary business often used in Boarding Facilities is a rider training program, or riding camps.

- <u>Horse Training</u> – "Horse Training" is training the horse, not the rider. This use is often combined with breeding and sales of horses. Location and facilities are important in success.

- <u>Rider Training</u> – Training the rider can be done for pleasure or it can be done for competition or events.

- <u>Breeding Farm / Animal Sales</u>- Although breeding farms are often horse farms as well, they could be cattle farms, pig farms, alpaca farms or any other type of animal.

- <u>Commercial Agricultural Farms / Agribusiness</u> – Growing any type of crop for public sale.

- <u>Timberland</u> – The timber industry, like any farming industry, locates or grows a crop and harvests that crop. Timberland is simply a specific type of crop.

# Business Opportunities

Selling a business is often more complicated than selling a commercial property or an office building. Purchasing any type of real estate is generally not a completely passive method of investing, however, purchasing an office building to rent to tenants is generally far more passive than purchasing a business that an investor may have to personally operate. While it is true that some businesses are sold complete with management and very little need for direct supervision by the investor, most require the investor to step in and make the business their career.

Some business opportunities include the real estate they occupy, and others simply include the equipment, name of the business, employees and "good will" of their past performance. Businesses are priced based on their Net Profits. Although many business owners would like the price to be based on their cost of equipment and inventory, as a real estate professional, you must understand that the buyer will not pay a price that will give the buyer no return or a negative return on their investment.

Business opportunities are generally categorized by a business category:

- <u>Retail Business</u> – like a Dunkin Donuts, a Jiffy Lube, a Laundry, or a Subway.

- <u>Professional Business</u>- such as a Dental Office or an Insurance Office. Because of licensure requirements, these are generally only purchased by buyers in those professions.

- <u>Distribution Business / Wholesale Business</u> – A distributor is the middleman between the manufacturer and the retailer. A distributor may buy truckloads of vegetables from farms and re-sell them to grocery stores, or purchase beverages directly from the maker and distribute them to restaurants.

- <u>Manufacturing Business</u> – The creation or production of anything to be sold.

Each type of business has a Standard Industrial Classification Code or SIC. When marketing a business, commercial realtors will often first contact owners of similar SIC categories to determine if the business is a good fit for others to absorb into their current portfolio.


## Important Questions to ask any Business Owner considering selling

Before a buyer leaps into the purchase of a business, they should have a clear picture of how the business operates. For example, in the salon industry, customers tend to stay with a particular stylist. If the owner has great income on her books, but has recently lost her 3 top stylists to other salons, the business could be in trouble. Analyze the customer base and whether the market for the business is growing, declining or remaining stable.

- Who are you selling to? Directly to consumers or to distributors and wholesalers?

- What is your approximate number of customers?

- Do any of your customers account for more than 10% of your annual business?

- Do you only sell locally, or are you regional or national?

- What is the trend of your market (increasing, stable or declining)?

- How do you promote or market your products or services?

- Why are you considering selling your business or company?

## Considering a business's SWOT

SWOT is an acronym for the Strengths, Weaknesses, Opportunities and Threats of any business. When a buyer is making a decision to change their life by taking over and running someone else's company or business, they want a very clear picture of what to expect.

- **Strengths** – Clear definition of the business strengths. This includes the location of the business, the employees or sales force, the product line and the efficiency of the operation.

- **Weaknesses** – Clear definition of what challenges exist in the same areas as the business strengths.

- **Opportunities** – In what way would the current owner change or improve the company? Why isn't this being done currently? Are there any markets that can be expanded? Can a new market be captured?

- **Threats** – Is a competitor considering opening nearby? Is a key employee retiring? Is there a decline in demand for your product or service?

## Vacant Developable Land

Vacant land can refer to any size vacant property, from a single in-town lot to a several hundred acre parcel. As commercial real estate brokers and agents, our interest in vacant parcels of land is generally for one of two types of prospects. The first type is an investment speculator who is looking to buy land and hold it for some period of time. A speculator is generally someone who has an expectation that the value of the property will increase more rapidly than inflation and provide a return on investment at some future date. This is a highly risky investment and must be carefully considered by the investor.

The second, and more prevalent, type of investor looking for raw or vacant land is one who wants to develop the property into some form of commercial use. The investor may be looking to build a multifamily housing project or office building in order to rent the property and create a return. Other possibilities are that the investor may be looking to build a condominium project and sell it off to create a quick return, or the investor may be looking to build a specific kind of business, such as a hotel or a golf course.

Whatever use the buyer or investor desires to develop, as a realtor, you must research the zoning of each property to find property that lends itself to that use. If the buyer is looking to develop a warehouse in a particular area, then you must determine which zoning codes allow warehouses and locate properties for sale in those zones, or find owners willing to sell property in those zones. Remember that you are never limited to those properties that are actively available. A good site locator will contact land owners in areas that are most advantageous to their buyers or investors.

## Senior Housing / Long Term Care Facilities

A great variety of long term housing exists for the elderly and those who need constant care. Commercial housing facilities are purchased by both investors looking for a return, as well as, health care professionals looking for a business to manage and maintain. Regulations vary from state to state and the industry is heavily regulated by many agencies. If you are

representing a buyer or seller in the long term care industry, you should contact your state agencies and determine all the requirements necessary to transfer the property from one entity to another. In Pennsylvania, for example, the process requires inspections, certifications and often several months before the state will allow the sale and transfer to be completed.

Like multifamily housing and shopping centers, Long Term Care facilities are generally priced by their return on investment. Different levels of care require different commitments from both the owner of the facility and the management of the facility.

## Forms of Long Term Care Facilities include:

- Independent Living – Although this particular category may fall under multifamily housing as well, it refers to housing specifically designed for seniors, in which the resident does not need daily assistance with medical or personal care. As with multifamily housing, these may be low rise, mid rise or high rise.

- Assisted Living – Housing designed for individuals who need some ongoing assistance, but who do not need the medical care provided in a nursing home. Assisted living facilities are generally designed to allow a resident much of the freedom of independent living, but with the benefit of a safe environment with the assistance they need. Most assisted living facilities provide meals for the residents as well as other services including salons, activities and entertainment.

- CCRC / Life Care – A Continuing Care Retirement Community is a retirement community that provides medical and health care options for its residents, including an on-site skilled nursing unit. One of the primary benefits of a CCRC to the resident is the ability for a couple to stay together, should one of them need medical attention and supervision.

- Dementia Care – Dementia or Alzheimer's disease can result in the loss of skills for everyday living. A patient can be disoriented, have a reduction in their judgment, memory or function, or possess an altered emotional state. Special care units for dementia or Alzheimer's provide 24 hour care, or can provide period care, such as adult day care, for patients.

- Nursing Care / Nursing Homes - A facility that provides for residents with chronic illness or disability. Although Nursing Homes are generally focuses on the elderly, residents often include those who have difficulty with mobility or eating disorders.

## Key Terms for Long Term Care investment:

- <u>Operating Margins</u> – Income as a proportion of revenue available to service debt. The gross income before interest, taxes, amortization and depreciation, less the debt.

- <u>EBITDAR</u>- Earnings before taxes but after deducting reserves.

- <u>Occupancy Rate</u>- Although a more apt term might be Occupancy Level. Unlike most multifamily housing, which tend to lease apartments for long periods of time, many long term care facilities have a constant flow of residents in and out of the facility. Residents may need more care than a facility can provide, or they may pass away, or their health may improve. The Occupancy rate is calculated by determining the average number of residents per day during a particular period (generally a year) and multiplying that average by the number of days in the period.

More information can be obtained from the National Investment Center for Seniors Housing and Care Industry (NIC) at www.NIC.org, or through the American Association of Homes and Services for the Aging (AAHSA).

# Summary

Many specialties exist within the universe of commercial real estate sales, leasing and management. A Realtor may choose to specialize in one particular type of property and become a specialist, or may choose to attempt to handle all commercial transactions. The agent should first train to recognize and understand the various types of commercial real estate, and the nuances of each category.

# Chapter 1: Review Questions

1. Which of the following are not categories of commercial property?

   A. Office Buildings
   B. Shopping Centers
   C. Farms
   D. Timeshares
   E. Vacant Developable Land

2. True or False: While there are key elements in distinguishing classifications of office buildings, much of the classification process is subjective.

3. BOMA stands for:

   A. Business Offices and Maintenance Association
   B. Building Owners and Managers Association
   C. Business Office and Management Association
   D. Building Offices and Management Association.

4. Separately deeded office spaces within a building are called _____ _____.

5. True or False: Office Space measurement has been standardized and is measured the same everywhere in the United States.

6. Common Areas in an office building include all but the following:

   A. Hallways in between separately rented offices
   B. Elevators
   C. The Lobby for the Office Building
   D. Bathrooms within a unit
   E. Fire Staircases

7. True or False: A Lifestyle Center is a office building that provides exercise facilities, a restaurant and other lifestyle facilities to the tenants.

8. According to the International Council of Shopping Centers, Open Air Shopping Centers include all of the following except:

   A. Theme or Festival Center
   B. Outlet Center

C.  Power Center
D.  Neighborhood Center
E.  All of the Above are Open Air Centers

9.    True or False:  Producing and processing of products and raw materials is considered a light industrial use.

10.   True or False:  Brownfields are typically unused industrial properties on the outskirts of town.

11.   In the field of Hospitality Real Estate, RevPAR is short for _____
_____  _____  _____

12.   True or False:  Tier two hotels tend to be older hotels in urban areas.

13.   All of the following are examples of multi family housing except:

A.  Duplexes
B.  Cooperatives
C.  Private Residence Clubs
D.  Residential Condominiums
E.  Mobile Home Parks

14.   A Gross Income Multiplier equals:

A.  The Sales Price divided by the income after expenses.
B.  The Sales Price divided by the Gross Income.
C.  The Scheduled Gross Income divided by the Sales Price.
D.  The Scheduled Gross Income divided by the number of units.

15.   Net Operating Income equals:

A.  The Gross Income minus the Operating Expenses.
B.  The Effective Gross Income minus the Operating Expenses.
C.  The Effective Gross Income minus the Operating Expenses and the annual Debt Service (principal and interest payments)
D.  The Gross Income minus the Operating Expenses and the Debt Service (principal and interest payments)
E.  The Net Profit minus the annual Debt Service (principal and interest payments)

16. The SWOT of a Business Opportunity analysis refers to the

    A. Strengths, Weaknesses, Operating Income and Time a business has been in operation.
    B. Sales figures, Workforce analysis, Operating Income and Time a business has been in operation.
    C. Sales figures, Workforce analysis, Opportunities and Threats of a business.
    D. Strengths, Weaknesses, Opportunities and Threats of a business.

17. True or False: Independent Living may fall under both the Multi Family category of commercial property and the Senior Housing category of commercial property.

18. True or False: Many Assisted Living Facilities provide the residents with meals, salon access, activities and entertainment, but the residents maintain the freedom of independent living.

19. EBITDAR is defined as _____ _____ _____
   _____ _____ _____ _____ _____.

20. True or False: Horse Boarding Facilities are not considered commercial properties.

# 2

# Data Gathering and Property Analysis

## Gathering Data

I've always believed that far too many of the training systems available for commercial real estate sales and leasing focus primarily on salesmanship (or salespersonship) and ignore the importance of research and analysis. In the field of commercial real estate sales and leasing, you are often handling an individual or company's most valuable assets. Take the time and care to understand what you are marketing, and how it fits into the current marketplace, so that you can properly advise your clients.

Whether you're working on behalf of a property owner attempting to sell a property, or a property buyer, user or investor considering making a purchase, you need to understand the potential value of the property.

There are several components to researching a property. As we'll discuss in detail in chapter 3, gathering and analyzing income information is one critical factor in pricing and selling properties. We also must research the zoning and potential uses of the property, and direct comparison of the property to similar properties in the area.

Other factors that affect the sales price and marketability of the property include competing properties in the marketplace demographic shifts, the economy and its impact on the property, and

| Researching a Property |
|---|
| • Income Data and Analysis |
| • Zoning Data and potential uses |
| • Direct Comparison with other properties |
| • Economic and Demographic Data and how it will impact the property |
| • Financing Availability |

availability of financing for the property. These factors will be broken down over the next few pages, and we'll examine why each is important in evaluating and marketing a property.

## Gathering Information

Before we can analyze the strengths and weaknesses of a particular property, we must first collect all the information we can about the property. Some of the information will come from tax records, but most will come from interviewing the property owner in person or over the phone.

The information you gather is the key to pricing the property correctly and determining the properties highest and best use. Each category of property, such as office, retail or industrial, has different key elements that you must gather. The following pages are samples of the data gathering forms my team uses to collect information about a property. The forms are based partly on property type.

Some information, such as expenses and lease terms, should be verified by obtaining copies of all documents from the property owner. If you are listing a property, request that the owner provide copies of all documents within a week of the listing. This will assist you in marketing the property, and assist you in portraying the property accurately.

If you are working on behalf of a buyer, you should make any offer conditioned on the seller providing copies of all income and expense documentation, leases and any other pertinent information. You should then build into any offer a due diligence period for the buyer to review these documents to their satisfaction.

Other information used for analyzing a property must be obtained from local municipalities, taxing authorities and zoning and planning departments. When researching an office building, if possible, obtain a copy of the floor plan of the building and a plot plan showing where the building and parking are located on the property. When researching a retail property or shopping center, obtain a

2 Unit Office Building with private entrances.

copy of the floor plans for the property, and a plot plan or survey showing where the building or buildings and parking areas are located on the property.

## Office Building Information Form

**Property Address:** _____

**Description of Building:**
Building Class (A,B,C): _____
Total Square Footage: _____
Number of Units: _____
Number of Floors: _____
Age of Building: _____
Most Recently Renovated: _____
Construction Type: _____
Elevator: _____
Overhead Doors: _____
Separate Utilities: _____
Type of Heating: _____
Electric _____
Water / Sewer: _____
Window Type: _____
Security Sys / Sprinkler?

**Site Description:**
Zoning of Property: _____
Lot Size: _____
Lot Frontage: _____
Number of Parking Spaces: _____
Location: _____

**Comments**
_____
_____
_____
_____
_____
_____
_____
_____
_____
_____
_____

**Unit Information:**
Rental Rate (psf): _____
Useable Square Footage: _____
CAM fees: _____
Lease Expiration: _____
Escalations? _____
Other Fees: _____

**Unit Information:**
Rental Rate (psf): _____
Useable Square Footage: _____
CAM fees: _____
Lease Expiration: _____
Escalations? _____
Other Fees: _____

**Unit Information:**
Rental Rate (psf): _____
Useable Square Footage: _____
CAM fees: _____
Lease Expiration: _____
Escalations? _____
Other Fees: _____

**Unit Information:**
Rental Rate (psf): _____
Useable Square Footage: _____
CAM fees: _____
Lease Expiration: _____
Escalations? _____
Other Fees: _____

**Unit Information:**
Rental Rate (psf): _____
Useable Square Footage: _____
CAM fees: _____
Lease Expiration: _____

# Office Building Information Form

**Property Address:** _____

| **Description of Building:** | | **Unit Information:** | |
|---|---|---|---|
| Building Class (A,B,C): | Class A | Rental Rate (psf): | $16 |
| Total Square Footage: | 11,838 | Useable Square Footage: | 3,550 |
| Number of Units: | 5 | CAM fees: | $2.50 |
| Number of Floors: | 2 | Lease Expiration: | 1/1/2013 |
| | | | Yearly - |
| Age of Building: | 5 Years | Escalations? | $1.00 |
| Most Recently Renovated: | N/A | Other Fees: | None |
| Construction Type: | Brick over steel frame | | |
| Elevator: | 1 Elevator | **Unit Information:** | |
| Overhead Doors: | None | Rental Rate (psf): | $15.50 |
| Separate Utilities: | Elec, Heat | Useable Square Footage: | 2,480 |
| Type of Heating: | Gas Hot Air | CAM fees: | $2.50 |
| Electric | Separated | Lease Expiration: | 4/1/2009 |
| Water / Sewer: | Public - Owner Paid | Escalations? | Yearly |
| Window Type: | Double Hung | Other Fees: | None |
| Security Sys / Sprinkler? | Sec Sys & Sprinkler | | |

| **Site Description:** | | **Unit Information:** | |
|---|---|---|---|
| | | Rental Rate (psf): | $16.50 |
| | | Useable Square Footage: | 2,200 |
| Zoning of Property: | Office Park | CAM fees: | $2.25 |
| Lot Size: | 1.33 Acres | Lease Expiration: | 6/1/2009 |
| Lot Frontage: | 225 feet | Escalations? | None |
| Number of Parking Spaces: | 48 | Other Fees: | None |
| Location: | Business Park | | |

| **Comments** | | **Unit Information:** | |
|---|---|---|---|
| | | Rental Rate (psf): | $17.00 |
| Really sharp building with | tile foyer, 2 sets of | Useable Square Footage: | 1,020 |
| stairs, elevator.  1st floor is | leased to a bank with | CAM fees: | $2.50 |
| 5 years on the lease.  CAM | fees include taxes, | Lease Expiration: | 10/1/2009 |
| insurance, maintenance, | water, sewer. | Escalations? | None |
| CAT 5 wire throughout the | building. | Other Fees: | None |
| Security System installed. | | | |

| **Unit Information:** | |
|---|---|
| Rental Rate (psf): | $16.50 |
| Useable Square Footage: | 1,080 |
| CAM fees: | $2.25 |
| Lease Expiration: | 2/1/2009 |
| Escalations? | None |

# Retail / Shopping Center Information Form

**Property Address:** _____

**Description of Building:**
Type of Building: _____
Total Square Footage: _____
Number of Units: _____
Number of Floors: _____
Age of Building: _____
Most Recently Renovated: _____
Construction Type: _____
Elevator: _____
Overhead Doors: _____
Separate Utilities: _____
Type of Heating: _____
Electric _____
Water / Sewer: _____
Window Type: _____
Security Sys / Sprinkler? _____
Days / Hours Open: _____

**Site Description:**
Zoning of Property: _____
Lot Size: _____
Lot Frontage: _____
Number of Parking
Spaces: _____
Location: _____
Traffic Count: _____

**Comments**
_____
_____
_____
_____
_____
_____
_____
_____
_____
_____

**Unit Information:**
Rental Rate (psf): _____
Useable Square Footage: _____
CAM fees: _____
Lease Expiration: _____
Escalations? _____
Other Fees: _____

**Unit Information:**
Rental Rate (psf): _____
Useable Square Footage: _____
CAM fees: _____
Lease Expiration: _____
Escalations? _____
Other Fees: _____

**Unit Information:**
Rental Rate (psf): _____
Useable Square Footage: _____
CAM fees: _____
Lease Expiration: _____
Escalations? _____
Other Fees: _____

**Unit Information:**
Rental Rate (psf): _____
Useable Square Footage: _____
CAM fees: _____
Lease Expiration: _____
Escalations? _____
Other Fees: _____

**Unit Information:**
Rental Rate (psf): _____
Useable Square Footage: _____
CAM fees: _____
Lease Expiration: _____
Escalations? _____
Other Fees:

# Industrial / Warehouse Information Form

**Property Address:** _____

| **Description of Building:** | | **Unit Information:** | |
|---|---|---|---|
| Type of Building: | _____ | Rental Rate (psf): | _____ |
| Total Square Footage: | _____ | Useable Square Footage: | _____ |
| Number of Floors: | _____ | CAM fees: | _____ |
| Age of Building: | _____ | Lease Expiration: | _____ |
| Most Recently Renovated: | _____ | Escalations? | _____ |
| Construction Type: | _____ | Other Fees: | _____ |
| Elevator: | _____ | | |
| Ceiling Heights: | _____ | **Unit Information:** | |
| Overhead Doors: | _____ | Rental Rate (psf): | _____ |
| Loading Docks: | _____ | Useable Square Footage: | _____ |
| Columns? | _____ | CAM fees: | _____ |
| Type of Heating and where: | _____ | Lease Expiration: | _____ |
| Air Conditioning? Location: | _____ | Escalations? | _____ |
| Electric Amerage | _____ | Other Fees: | _____ |
| Water (Pub, Well) / Line Size | _____ | | |
| Sewer (Public, Septic) | _____ | **Unit Information:** | |
| Window Type: | _____ | Rental Rate (psf): | _____ |
| Security Sys / Sprinkler? | _____ | Useable Square Footage: | _____ |
| Underground Tanks? | _____ | CAM fees: | _____ |
| Restrooms? | _____ | Lease Expiration: | _____ |
| | | Escalations? | _____ |
| **Site Description:** | | Other Fees: | _____ |
| Zoning of Property: | _____ | | |
| Lot Size: | _____ | **Unit Information:** | |
| Lot Frontage: | _____ | Rental Rate (psf): | _____ |
| Number of Parking Spaces: | _____ | Useable Square Footage: | _____ |
| Location: | _____ | CAM fees: | _____ |
| | | Lease Expiration: | _____ |
| | | Escalations? | _____ |
| **Comments** _____ | | Other Fees: | _____ |
| _____ | | | |
| _____ | | **Unit Information:** | |
| _____ | | Rental Rate (psf): | _____ |
| _____ | | Useable Square Footage: | _____ |
| _____ | | CAM fees: | _____ |
| _____ | | Lease Expiration: | _____ |
| _____ | | Escalations? | |

# Multifamily Information Form

**Property Address:** _____

**Description of Building(s):**
Type of Multifamily: _____
Total # Units _____
# of occupied Units _____
Age of Building(s): _____
Most Recently Renovated: _____
Construction Type: _____
Elevator: _____
Heating Type _____
Air Conditioning? _____
Electric Amerage Per Unit _____
Water (Pub, Well) / Line Size _____
Sewer (Public, Septic) _____
Security Sys / Sprinkler? _____
Tenant Paid Utilities: _____

_____

Landlord Paid Utilities: _____

_____
_____
_____
_____

**Site Description:**
Zoning of Property: _____
Lot Size: _____
Lot Frontage: _____
Number of Parking Spaces: _____
Location: _____

**Comments** _____
_____
_____
_____
_____
_____
_____

**Unit Information:**
Number of 1 Bedrooms: _____
Number of 2 Bedrooms: _____
Number of 3 Bedrooms: _____
Number of 4 Bedrooms: _____
Number of Efficiencies: _____
Other Units: _____

**Breakdown of Rents**
Unit 1 _____
Unit 2 _____
Unit 3 _____
Unit 4 _____
Unit 5 _____
Unit 6 _____
Unit 7 _____
Unit 8 _____
Unit 9 _____
Unit 10 _____
Unit 11 _____
Unit 12 _____
Unit 13 _____
Unit 14 _____
Unit 15 _____

# Multifamily Unit Detail Form

**Property Address:** _____

---

**Unit #**

| | | | |
|---|---|---|---|
| Unit Description: | _____ | Rental Rate: | _____ |
| | _____ | Occupied? | _____ |
| # Bedrooms & Baths | _____ | Expiration Date of Lease: | _____ |
| Appliances included: | | Tenant Paid Utilities: | |

---

**Unit #**

| | | | |
|---|---|---|---|
| Unit Description: | _____ | Rental Rate: | _____ |
| | _____ | Occupied? | _____ |
| # Bedrooms & Baths | _____ | Expiration Date of Lease: | _____ |
| Appliances included: | | Tenant Paid Utilities: | |

---

**Unit #**

| | | | |
|---|---|---|---|
| Unit Description: | _____ | Rental Rate: | _____ |
| | _____ | Occupied? | _____ |
| # Bedrooms & Baths | _____ | Expiration Date of Lease: | _____ |
| Appliances included: | | Tenant Paid Utilities: | |

---

**Unit #**

| | | | |
|---|---|---|---|
| Unit Description: | _____ | Rental Rate: | _____ |
| | _____ | Occupied? | _____ |
| # Bedrooms & Baths | _____ | Expiration Date of Lease: | _____ |
| Appliances included: | | Tenant Paid Utilities: | |

---

**Unit #**

| | | | |
|---|---|---|---|
| Unit Description: | _____ | Rental Rate: | _____ |
| | _____ | Occupied? | _____ |
| # Bedrooms & Baths | _____ | Expiration Date of Lease: | _____ |
| Appliances included: | | Tenant Paid Utilities: | |

---

**Unit #**

| | | | |
|---|---|---|---|
| Unit Description: | _____ | Rental Rate: | _____ |
| | _____ | Occupied? | _____ |
| # Bedrooms & Baths | _____ | Expiration Date of Lease: | _____ |
| Appliances included: | | Tenant Paid Utilities: | |

If the property is leased, has lease potential or generates an income stream from something other than a specific business, you'll need to gather information about the income and operating expenses of the property. The form below is a simple version of an Income and Expense Form.

## Income and Expenses

**Income:**
Gross Rental Income  _____
CAM Fees  _____
Taxes paid by tenants  _____
Utilities paid by tenants  _____
Less Vacancy  _____
Gross Rental Income less vacancy  _____
Additional Income (Laundry, Soda, etc)  _____
**Gross Income**  _____

**Operating Expenses:**
Real Estate Taxes  _____
Property Insurance  _____
Liability Insurance  _____
Utilities: Electric  _____
Utilities: Heating  _____
Utilities: Water  _____
Utilities: Sewer  _____
Garbage / Refuse  _____
Maintenance  _____
Property Management  _____
Professional Services  _____
Security  _____
**Total Operating Expenses**  _____

**Net Operating Income**  _____

---

## Hospitality Property Information Form

**Property Address:** _____

**Description of Building:**
Hotel Grade (Tier 1,2,3,4):  _____
Franchise:  _____
Total Square Footage:  _____
Number of Guest Rooms:  _____
Number of Suites:  _____
Number of Floors:  _____
Age of Building:  _____
Most Recently Renovated:  _____
Construction Type:  _____
Elevator:  _____
Type of Heating:  _____
Electric  _____
Water / Sewer:  _____
Window Type:  _____
Security Sys / Sprinkler?  _____

**Guest Mix:**
% Convention:  _____
% Business Traveler:  _____
% Tourist:  _____
% Other:  _____

**Calculations:**
Yearly Avg Occupancy:  _____
Yearly ADR:  _____

**Staff:**
Number of Employees:  _____
Wage / Salary expense:  _____

**Other Income Sources:**
Restaurant  _____
Weddings / Functions  _____
Other  _____

**Site Description:**
Zoning of Property:  _____
Lot Size:  _____
Lot Frontage:  _____
Number of Parking Spaces:  _____
Location:  _____

**Comments**
_____
_____
_____
_____
_____
_____
_____
_____

---

Obviously with a hospitality property, you'll need significantly more information, but this is a start for analyzing the property.

# Zoning Data and Potential Uses

When studying a property, you may find that the current use of the property is probably its highest and best use. That means that the property is likely to generate a better return for the owner or the buyer by keeping the same use. You may find, however, that the corner garage you're listing might be better suited as a mini-mart. Perhaps you determine that the buildings on the property could be expanded to allow for more leasable space or even a secondary use on the same property.

There are many real estate professionals who have made themselves very wealthy by researching property and determining how to maximize the income from a property by altering the property use. Zoning may allow a zoning change or special exception to tear down an old warehouse in a high traffic location in lieu of a shopping center with much higher rental rates.

## Zoning Regulations

Zoning committees or zoning hearing boards throughout the country create regulations or codes for their particular municipalities. Most townships, towns, boroughs, and cities have zoning maps that allocate parts of their geographic area to different uses. These rules and regulations establish the possible uses of any property in the area, as well as, restrictions on those uses such as setbacks from the main road and maximum building size or height.

Although some parts of the country are pro-growth and have very liberal zoning regulations, far more areas have very restrictive zoning regulations in order to restrict growth. My experience has been that zoning hearing boards tend to attract those individuals who want to keep the "status quo" and prevent or control the growth in an area. In some states, the state or county has the right to restrict the rules written by zoning boards and requires boards to set aside land for various uses, such as commercial, multifamily and industrial.

Zoning codes vary widely from municipality to municipality. Don't be fooled by the similarities in zoning code names and symbols. Each municipality's zoning regulation or code manual lays out all the various zoning forms in that municipality and what uses are permitted in each zone. For example, a municipality may have 5 levels of residential zoning, labeled R1 through R5. Each level may allow for a different minimum lot size, different minimum road frontage and different setbacks. R1 might allow attached townhomes on minimum lots of 6000 square feet that sit back a minimum of 25 feet from the road. R2 might allow for single family homes on minimum quarter acre lots that require a 30 foot distance from the road, while R5 requires single family homes to be on a minimum of 10 acres.

Most zoning regulations also allow conditional uses and special exceptions in addition to the permitted uses in any particular zone.

- **Permitted Use** – The owner may use the property for any use that is permitted under this heading. In many areas, the owner may simply need a permit to begin construction, but does not need zoning approval.

- **Conditional Use** – The owner may use the property for a conditional use at the discretion of the zoning hearing board. The owner must make an application to the board for the conditional use. Prospective buyers or tenants of a property may make an offer on the property conditioned upon an approval for a conditional use from the zoning board.

- **Special Exception** – A special exception may require a more detailed plan to be submitted to a municipal zoning board than a conditional use proposal. Special exception hearings may require an owner to show a hardship, or notify neighbors and speak before a public meeting.

- **Grandfathered Use** - If a commercial use is forbidden in a particular zone, but a commercial use has existed in the property for a long period of time, the zoning board generally grandfather's the use. Some businesses have been in existence longer than the enactment of zoning codes.

- **Spot Zoning** – If a zoning board allows a property to be used for a purpose other than what the zoning code allows, it is referred to as spot zoning. For example, a zoning board may allow an accountant or lawyer to practice out of their home in a zone that forbids a commercial use. In some areas of the country, courts have found spot zoning to be illegal.

## Restrictions on Building

As you work with buyers who are considering building their dream building on a vacant lot, or tearing down another building to build theirs, you'll discover many varied restrictions in addition to the zoning usage. Setbacks restrict the building envelope on the property and maximum height restrictions limit the height of the building. A property may be limited by how much land may be covered by the building, or limited even by the parking requirements of a municipality. You will have to work carefully with engineers and architects to determine what can be built on a particular property and how large the buildings may be.

## Setbacks

Zoning codes often establish a minimum distance for any dwelling or building from the road, and any adjoining properties. These minimum distance requirements may be different for the distance from the street, distance from sides of the lot, and distance from the rear of the property. For example, setbacks from the road in front may be 25 feet, 15 feet from the sides of the property and 20 feet from the rear of the property. Setbacks create a building envelope in which you may construct your home or building.

Additional setbacks may exist from major roads or intersections. Zoning codes may restrict a building close to a major corner in order to allow for maximum visibility for drivers on that corner. Business signs are often restricted with setbacks in the same fashion.

## Set Backs

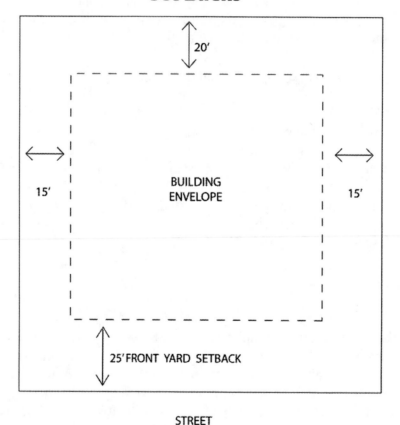

56

## ...ight Restrictions

...codes forbid construction over a certain height, depending on the use of the
...eight restrictions can be in place because the local fire departments may not
...quipment to handle buildings over a certain height, or they may be in place to
...e neighboring property views. Exceptions may be made by zoning boards for
...towers, amusement park rides, and similar uses.

## Site Coverage

In commercial and industrial uses, zoning regulations may exist that restrict the size of
the building or parking areas based on the size of the lot. For example, one zoning board
has passed a code that restricts the building footprint to a maximum of 25% of the size of
the lot, and the "hard coat coverage" to a maximum of 45% of the size of the lot. Hard
Coat generally refers to any surface impervious to water penetration, and includes the
building, any parking lot area and any concrete pads or other impervious surfaces. If a
client has an industrial site containing 1 acre, or 43,560 square feet, they are restricted to
a maximum of 10,890 square feet on the first floor of the building. The owners are
further restricted to a maximum of 19,602 square feet of coverage of the property.

Example:

Lot Size: 1 Acre = 43,560 Square Feet
Maximum First Floor Space = 25% Coverage of Lot Size = .25 x 43,560 = 10,890
Maximum Impervious Coverage = 45% of Lot Size = .45 x 43,560 = 19,602
Maximum Parking Area = 19,602 – 10,890 = 8,712

## Parking Restrictions

Zoning codes will also require a minimum number of parking spaces, based on the
building size and the use of the property. For example, a particular municipality may
require 3 parking spaces for each 1000 square feet of office space, or 5 parking spaces for
each 1000 square feet of retail space. The variation is generally based on the estimated
number of employees and customers that might be using the space.

Parking spaces are commonly 10 feet by 20 feet and require a clearance of 20 feet behind in order to back out of the space. Most office and retail parking lots create aisles of spaces facing each other so that spaces across from each other can share the "back-out" area, allowing the planner to set aside 300 square feet per parking space (10 feet by 30 feet, sharing the aisle).

Building size may be further limited by the parking requirements. Using the same example under site coverage, if a township requires 3 parking spaces per 1,000 square feet of office space, and your client wants to build a single story office building, the building size may have to be

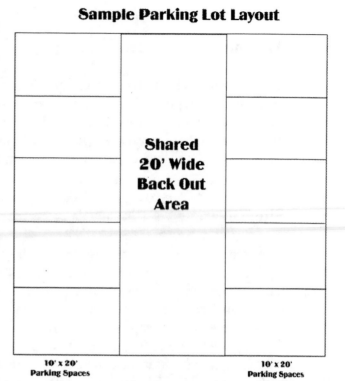

**Sample Parking Lot Layout**

Shared
20' Wide
Back Out
Area

10' x 20'
Parking Spaces

10' x 20'
Parking Spaces

reduced in order to allow for parking. In the prior example, 25% building coverage was 10,890 square feet. That would require 37 parking spaces, which would take up a minimum of 11,100 square feet (based on 300 square feet per space), which is larger than the maximum remaining area. The building may have to be reduced to 10,000 square feet in order to make the calculation work.

---

Example:

Lot Size: 1 Acre = 43,560 Square Feet
Maximum Impervious Coverage = 45% of Lot Size = .45 x 43,560 = 19,602
3 Spaces per 1,000 Square Feet = 900 sq ft Parking per 1,000 sq ft Building
10,000 sq ft Building x (900 sq ft parking per 1,000 sq ft building) = 9,000
10,000 sq ft building + 9,000 sq ft parking = 19,000 sq ft total

---

## Improvements

Zoning boards may also require an individual or company that is building a new shopping center, office building or complex to make improvements to the area's surrounding infrastructure. A developer may be required to add a traffic light to an adjacent or nearby intersection. They may be required to make a payment to the local fire department for additional personnel that an office complex may require in the event of an emergency. Utility lines in the area may have to be enlarged in order to service the new project, at the cost of the developer.

Although every possibility cannot be predicted by any realtor, engineer or developer, a basic understanding of what type of improvements may be required and what costs for improvements may be incurred by the developer is critical to pricing the property correctly.

# Understanding the Market Area

A primary function in commercial real estate sales is evaluation of property. In some cases, we are evaluating a property for an owner who wishes to sell or lease the property for top dollar. In others, we are evaluating a property on behalf of a buyer or tenant who doesn't want to pay more than market value for the purchase or lease of a property. This is complicated by the fact that the current use of the property may not be the highest and best possible use of the property.

In order to fully understand the current value and the potential value of any parcel, we have to gauge the strengths and weaknesses of the property in comparison with other similar properties that are either currently on the market or have recently sold. In addition to specific property data and comparison, we need to study the trends in the local economy to be able to accurately predict the best course of action for a property owner at this point in time.

## Research Specific to the Property

First, we must determine what is the "market area" for a particular property so that we can do a comparison of other properties in the same marketplace. The market area for real estate is generally a geographic area within a certain radius of the property. The radius may not be an exact circle, however. It may be bounded by certain landmarks or natural barriers. For example, in Philadelphia, office buildings along the Delaware River on the Pennsylvania side have significantly different rental rates than those on the New Jersey side a few hundred yards away. The river is a natural boundary. Boundaries may include major roads, highways, rivers, mountains, parks and more.

Determining a market area is critical to pricing because commercial property will be most affected by the sales and leasing of other commercial property in the same market area. The market area can be different for different types of property. For example, office buildings for lease may compete with other office buildings for lease in the same downtown business district with a radius of only a few blocks. In the same location, retail space may be affected by the lease of space 5 to 10 miles away at a major regional mall.

There are 3 market areas to consider. The directly competing properties are the <u>primary or immediate market</u> close to the subject property. These are the buildings or spaces that buyers or tenants are most likely to consider when they are viewing your property. The second market is aptly called the <u>secondary market</u> and includes those properties that, although are not directly surrounding the seller's property, are generally also considered by prospective buyers and tenants.

The furthest market to consider in your evaluation is the <u>tertiary market</u> which includes properties that may be a significant distance from the property you are studying, but are also areas or properties that may be acceptable to tenants or buyers. For example, my team recently researched the rise in vacancy rate in a previously high occupancy retail area. We found that many prospective tenants were being drawn to a new "Lifestyle Center" 8 miles from the primary retail market. The tenants were being sold on the concept of a Lifestyle Center being built in a 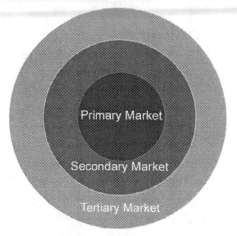 location that has previously not held any retail businesses. This was a move created in a tertiary market that significantly affected our primary market, driving some rental rates down.

It's also important to note that when you're comparing various properties as potential competition, you should use similar properties. When comparing office space, for example, Class A space should be compared primarily to other Class A space. A comparison between buildings of various ages and conditions may be helpful to show ranges based on classification, but direct comparison should be with very similar space.

When comparing retail properties, the primary, secondary and tertiary markets depend partly on the size of the retail property or shopping center. I generally consider the primary market for a retail property or shopping center property to be based on the radius that includes 75% of their customers.

Obviously, a small retail business would be likely to have a small primary radius of between 1 and 5 miles. With a Community Shopping Center or Neighborhood Shopping

Center, the primary market would be between 3 and 6 miles. A Lifestyle Center or Super Regional Center can have a primary marketplace that extends to 25 miles. Please keep in mind that shoppers are generally willing to drive 5 to 15 minutes for groceries or a pharmacy. They are willing to drive 15 minutes to a half hour for a regional mall. And they may be willing to drive an hour to get to a specialty store or outlet center.

A secondary market radius for retail should include another 20% of the business or shopping center's customers. The tertiary market radius includes the balance of customers, obviously with exception to those one time customers who may come from outside the area.

Industrial property comparisons should be made to sites that have similar amenities and locations. For example, a site that has access to rail service should be compared directly with other properties with rail service. Industrial property buyers often have greater latitude in area to consider. The immediate market for industrial may be an entire region, or the Metropolitan Statistical Area. The tertiary market could extend into several states that have access to highways or rail lines that will get the manufacturer's goods to the appropriate markets.

Special use properties, such as cold storage facilities or self storage facilities, should be compared directly against other properties with the same function.

## Where to find Property Comparison Data

Unlike residential property comparables, which can generally be found in the local multiple listing system, commercial real estate doesn't always make it into the local systems. Many agents and brokers keep their listings quiet. To get a true and accurate picture of what's happening in a marketplace, you'll need to do some leg work. Surveying and canvassing are a big component in building a database of comparables.

Because you will be adding data from several sources, you'll need to create a chart or spreadsheet of the properties you study, in order to easily compare and contrast them. For example, fields on your spreadsheet for an office sale may include list price, sales price, square footage, lot size, amenities, parking and notes.

If you're studying investment properties, your spreadsheet should certainly include list price, sales price, number of rental units, net operating income, and cap rate. An industrial property comparison may include ceiling height, number of overhead doors and rail / highway access.

I always suggest beginning with the MLS because you will often find enough information to begin your study of the market. Remember to select your specific primary market area first, and search for similar properties for lease and sale in that primary market. Plug those numbers into your spreadsheet.

Your second search should be of all the online sources you can find. That would include current listings and recent sales on commercial web databases like Loopnet, CoStar, Propertyline or Cityfeet. Again, you should add the most comparable properties to your spreadsheet.

Last, it's time to hit the pavement or the telephone. The best way to obtain data about a particular market is to simply visit or call property owners and tenants of similar properties. Survey the owners and tenants to find out the information you need. This is very time consuming, but data can be used over and over again if you specialize in a particular market and property type.

Other good sources of information include local commercial appraisers, who compile data on both leases and sales in an area, tax records, local chamber of commerce, local economic development organizations, local zoning and planning commission members, commercial finance organizations and commercial bankers.

## Comparisons for investment properties

Chapter 4 will deal specifically with understanding investment properties and their returns. At the point of gathering and analyzing data on an investment property, make sure you find out the exact income and expenses, the number of units and the amenities of the property. One example of a short investment property survey is shown below:

| Investment Property Survey | | | | | | | |
|---|---|---|---|---|---|---|---|
| Address | List Price | Sales Price | Days on Mkt | Units | Price / Unit | NOI | Cap Rate |
| 15 Berger Way | $459,900 | $452,000 | 96 | 10 | 45,200 | $44,200.00 | 10.23 |
| 127 Alberdeen Rd | $375,000 | $372,000 | 28 | 8 | 46,500 | $36,500.00 | 10.19 |
| 19 Scotts Drive | $499,900 | $470,000 | 115 | 10 | 47,000 | $45,000.00 | 10.44 |
| 78 2nd Avenue | $325,000 | $310,000 | 34 | 7 | 44,286 | $29,100.00 | 10.65 |
| 783 Andover Road | $429,000 | $415,000 | 19 | 8 | 51,875 | $38,800.00 | 10.7 |
| 11 Bittner Way | $275,000 | $270,000 | 27 | 6 | 45,000 | $28,200.00 | 9.57 |

## Comparisons for office properties

Office properties are purchased by both users and by investors, so it's important to analyze the property from both perspectives. There are three major methods to comparing office buildings:

1. **Comparison by Building and Amenities**- Key components of comparing an office building or complex to other buildings include the classification of the building (A, B, or C), the façade of the building, the building size and its age. Amenities of the building should be factored into the equation. Amenities include the amount of parking, computer lines and technology, security, elevators, as well as any health club access or similar features.

2. **Comparison by Income and Rental** – What are buyers and investors paying for properties with similar net incomes? What is the vacancy rate of this building in relation to others in the area? What types of leases are on this property compared to others (triple net, or gross?) and how is the property currently managed?

3. **Comparison by Location** – Office buildings close to parks, shopping, transportation and restaurants tend to be more easily leased to tenants. Location can play a key role in a buyer or investor selecting one building over another, and is generally key to a tenant selecting one space over another.

Example of Office Building Survey spreadsheet:

## Office Property Survey

| Address | List Price | Sales Price | Sq Ft | Lot Size | NOI | Price Per SF | Cap Rate |
|---|---|---|---|---|---|---|---|
| 55 Potter Highway | $1,200,000 | $1,020,000 | 10,280 | 1.3 Ac | $91,200 | $99.22 | 11.18 |
| 1 Industrial Plaza | $1,500,000 | $1,460,000 | 15,260 | 1.6 Ac | $152,700 | $95.67 | 9.56 |
| 77 Scotsdale Court | $2,100,000 | $1,980,000 | 21,580 | 2.2 Ac | $210,780 | $91.75 | 9.39 |
| 1957 Independence | $995,000 | $965,000 | 8,200 | 1.1 Ac | $96,500 | $117.68 | 10.00 |
| 31 Main Street | $1,750,000 | $1,630,000 | 16,300 | 2.1 Ac | $171,851 | $100.00 | 9.48 |
| 82 Bixloxi Blvd | $1,450,000 | $1,310,000 | 12,550 | 1.3 Ac | $141,600 | $104.38 | 9.25 |

## Comparisons for Retail properties and Shopping Centers

Retail sites are often purchased or leased by users. Shopping centers, strip malls and retail complexes are purchased by investors or investment groups. In both cases, the primary considerations are proximity to population, traffic count and the physical "look" of the property.

When making a comparison of retail sites and shopping centers, your spreadsheet should account for more than just the investment component. How long ago was the center renovated? What is the vacancy rate of the property and the mix of tenants? How strong are the major anchor stores?

1. **Comparison by Center and Amenities** - Key components of comparing a shopping center to other centers include the age of the center, the façade or modernization of the building, the building size, the major anchor stores, the mix of tenants and the proximity of parking to the actual stores.

2. **Comparison by Income and Rental** – What are buyers and investors paying for centers with similar net incomes? What is the vacancy rate of this center in relation to others in the area? What types of leases are on this property compared to others, and what are the current CAM fees?

3. **Comparison by Location** – In any retail business, making the business visible to the public is one of the most important aspects of choosing a location. Traffic count and distance to major highways is a primary consideration to any shopping center or retail property. Accessibility to the property, and the ability to easily enter and exit the property add to the value.

## Comparisons for Industrial properties and Warehouse properties

Like Office Buildings or Retail properties, Industrial properties can be sold to users or to investors. Users may pay a different price for a property based on their needs and the property amenities than an investor. The permitted uses under zoning and the location in comparison to rail service, major highways, and the businesses clients play key roles in choosing a site.

If you are attempting to determine the likely sales price of a cold storage facility, you must compare the facility to other cold storage facilities that may be within driving distance of the property. Industrial properties with access to cranes, rail roads and rail loading should be compared with similar properties.

Key comparison factors include size of building, ceiling heights, lot size or site size, floor load limits and type of construction. Agents listing industrial properties should also be conscious of possible environmental issues such as buried storage tanks, waste removal, and any sort of dumping on the property.

## Research on the Marketplace

Once you have a solid handle on the current pricing of property in the area, you'll need to forecast the direction of the market by researching demographic trends and the marketplace. You are trying to advise a client of their best course of action with regard to their real estate holdings. It is important you have a full understanding of what is taking place in the local economy as well as nationally. For example, if your client owns a retail pad site next to a parcel of land that Wal-Mart is considering, your client might be best advised to wait to market the property for a few months. The announcement of a large retailer on an adjacent site can drive prices up. There is a slight warning, however. If you wait to list the property, other buyers may call your client directly.

If the market is sluggish currently, but you expect it to pull out shortly, it may be better to wait. If, on the other hand, interest rates are rising and the rental income on an investment property is not, the owner may consider pricing the property realistically so that the property sells before the property devalues.

Economic factors you should consider in your analysis include anything that can affect the supply of or demand for commercial property in your market area. Although a complete explanation of macroeconomics is beyond the scope of this text, you should be concerned with demographic trends, lifestyle trends, and absorption rates or vacancy rates in your market area.

One of the other key elements that you should understand when marketing commercial, office or industrial space is that you may be the first or the primary contact for a company considering buying or building a large office building, facility or manufacturing plant in your marketplace. Having a complete understanding of your marketplace is critical to selling it to prospective buyers. It is also important to understand key demographic information when selling property so you can better understand where to tailor your marketing efforts.

Some important key data to know and understand include:

- **Distances to Major Markets** – As you're trying to entice manufacturing facilities, distribution facilities or even offices and retail centers, you should be aware of the accessibility to other major population centers. Have a clear understanding of the highway system, rail system and distances to major markets.

- **Employment Information** – Unemployment rates, breakdown of major employers, workforce characteristics and income ranges of the local workforce can be important in attracting companies to an area. Understanding the workforce can also be important criteria when opening upscale shopping centers or retail outlets.

- **Employer Information**- An important consideration in any market is the breakdown of employers and makeup of local industries. For example, in coal mining areas, all property values decreased as coal production shut down, because many coal mining areas had only one major employer. Other businesses were related to the servicing of either the major industry or servicing the employees of the coal industry. A diverse group of employers in an area can help to ease downturns in any particular market.

- **Educational Institutions**- Many companies like to locate close to intellectual resources such as Universities and other institutes of higher learning. Areas with a significant number of colleges and universities tend to attract a highly educated population.

- **Area Amenities and Lifestyle**- Some companies have relocated to areas like Saint Louis, MO or San Antonio, TX because they appreciate the culture or the lifestyle. Demand in those areas increase as more industry or employers move into them, increasing the price of real estate. Lifestyle includes physical amenities like waterfront areas, parks, zoos, attractions and recreational activities. Lifestyle can also include some nebulous amenities like culture and architecture.

## Finding and Compiling Market Data

As with researching specific properties, market data can often be found both on the Internet and by canvassing or surveying local organizations and municipalities. Good sources of information locally include the chamber of commerce, local and state economic development organizations, zoning and planning commission members, the local newspaper, area employers, and local commercial bankers.

A great deal of demographic information and trend analysis is available free on the web. Every state in the country has its own website. Look through the state website and local government websites for reports and demographic information.

Online sources of information include:

## National Demographic Sources

- **United States Census Bureau** – www.census.gov – provides demographic information for the entire country.
- **United States Department of Commerce** – www.doc.gov – provides information on commerce and business.
- **United States Housing and Urban Development** – www.hud.gov – provides information on housing and the housing industry.

## Real Estate Information

- **National Association of Realtors** – www.realtor.org – provides a full library of information.
- **The Urban Land Institute** - www.uli.org – provides information and publications including information on shopping centers.
- **The Institute of Real Estate Management** – www.irem.org – provides publications and reports including analysis for multifamily housing.

## Other Useful Information Sources

- **Standard and Poor's** – www.standardpoor.com – Industry surveys.
- **Inman News** – www.inman.com - Real Estate news reports.

## Associations that provide reports and data

- **CCIM Institute**- Commercial Brokers. www.ccim.com
- **Appraisal Institute**- www.appraisalinstitute.com
- **BOMA**- www.boma.org – the Building Owners and Managers Association.
- **SIOR**- www.sior.com – Society of Industrial and Office Realtors.
- **IREM**- www.irem.org – Institute of Real Estate Management.
- **ICSC** – www.icsc.org – International Council of Shopping Centers.
- **NAREIT**- www.nareit.com – National Association of Real Estate Investment Trusts.

# Vacancy and Absorption Rates

The vacancy rate of a property is the percentage of space that is not currently rented at a point in time. Any property will have some vacancy at some point in time. Tenants will move to larger or smaller spaces, relocate, or go completely out of business.

For a multifamily property, the vacancy rate is typically the number of vacant units divided by the total number of units. This is usually calculated on an annual basis. For example, if a property contains 3 units, there are 36 rentable months (3 x 12 months). If 2 of them were vacant for 1 month each during the year, the vacancy rate would be 2 / 36 or 5.56%.

For office property, the vacancy rate is typically the square footage vacant divided by the total leasable square footage of the property. In retail, the vacancy rate is generally the square footage vacant divided by the total leasable square footage of the property, although it could be the number of commercial units vacant divided by the total number of commercial units, if there is no major anchor store.

---

**Vacancy Rates for an Individual Property**

Multifamily Vacancy Rate = Number of Vacant Units / Total Number of Units

Office Vacancy Rate = Vacant Square Footage / Gross Leasable Square Footage

Retail Vacancy Rate = Vacant Square Footage / Gross Square Footage

---

Vacancy is a critical factor in both selling and financing a commercial property. Buyers and investors in the marketplace purchasing multifamily properties, shopping centers and office buildings like to see a consistent stream of income from the property. If there is a high vacancy factor in any particular property, the buyer or investor is left to wonder what makes the property less desirable to prospective tenants, and will offer accordingly. Typically, when financing a property, lenders will not give full value to a property that is significantly empty.

When researching a property, you should attempt to determine the vacancy rate for a property category in the primary marketplace. If the vacancy rate in a particular sub-market, such as the warehouse market in a downtown area, significantly increases, the rental rates charged for that type of space tends to drop. Just like any supply and demand function, if there is a greater supply of available space, owners will compete for fewer tenants and offer incentives or drop their prices in order to attract those tenants. Of course, the income for the property suffers, and can adversely affect the value of the property.

## Factors that affect vacancy rates

- **Local Economic Cycles** - Vacancy rates often follow market cycles. In any particular demographic area, the local economy can positively or negatively affect the business cycle, which can lead to new business start-ups and business expansions, or to closing businesses and business contraction. The shut down of major employers in an area can also lead to higher vacancy rates as the suppliers of the employer also have a reduced need for space. Conversely, rapid growth in a particular market area could lead to a significant rise in the rental rates as demand grows for space and the supply of available space shrinks.

- **National Economy** – The national economy can significantly affect vacancy rates. For example, a rise in unemployment may lead to less people in the marketplace buying goods, which will lead to a slowdown in retail sales, and then a slowdown in the manufacture of those goods. A fall in unemployment may have the opposite effect.

- **New Construction of Competing Properties** – Overbuilding of any market segment can lead to higher vacancy. Developers often follow other developers. Many parts of the country have experienced overbuilding of everything from office buildings to residential dwellings. Investors or developers believe there may be a shortage of a particular type of space, and build more to capitalize on that shortage. Construction of new space tends to hurt the lease of existing space. An increase in supply, with demand holding steady, will tend to reduce the rental rates of the space, and increase the vacancy rate.

- **Financing Rates or Construction Prices for New Construction** – As financing rates drop, investors are more likely to build competing space. As financing rates increase, or the cost to build commercial space increase, the return on new space decreases, leading fewer investors to build. A reduction in the rate of growth of space can lead to less supply on the market to serve the demand, reducing the vacancy rate.

- **Anti Construction Sentiment** – The "Not In My Backyard" crowd exists throughout the country. As groups pressure zoning boards to limit, restrict or forbid the construction of new space, the demand for existing space increases, increasing the rental rates and reducing vacancy.

## Calculating Vacancy Rate for a Marketplace

In a perfect world, we'd be able to simply look up exactly what space is currently vacant in any market, what the average rental rates are, and what space in under construction. Unfortunately, we usually have to do a form of extrapolation. There are three methods for determining a market's vacancy rate, but only two are very practical.

1.   **Total Vacancy Rate using Property Surveying** – A method to determine the true and correct vacancy rate would be to locate all competing properties in the area and call or visit them to determine their current vacancy and overall square footage. In an office park, the method might call for contacting every owner of every property in the park to determine their vacancy rate and add up all available space, all vacant space and divide. This method is impractical because of the time it takes to survey and calculate the exact vacancy.

---

**Calculating Marketplace Vacancy Rates:**

Total Vacant Space in Market / Total Existing Space in Market = Market Vacancy Rate

---

2.   **Average Vacancy Rate** – The realtor or appraiser takes a representative sample of similar buildings in the same area and determines the vacancy rate for those buildings, and then calculates an average based on the vacancy rate of each individual property. This is a common method for determining a market vacancy rate, although it may be inaccurate depending on how the realtor or appraiser selects the properties.

3.   **Weighted Average Vacancy Rate** – As with the average vacancy rate, the realtor or appraiser must select a representative sample of properties from the particular market or sub-market, and calculate a weighted average of the rate of vacancy.

## Understanding Absorption Rates

Once you have an understanding of the rate of vacancy of a market or sub-market, you can then consider the rate at which the current inventory will be absorbed by the market.

Absorption rates are important to investors building new inventory in a market. Developers and investors want an estimate of how long it may take to fill a building.

To calculate the absorption in a particular market, you must find out what the total vacant space was at the beginning of a time period, and the total vacant space now. For example, if there were 180,000 square feet of Class A office space available for lease at the beginning of the year, and 155,000 square feet of Class A office space available at the end of the year, 25,000 square feet was absorbed by the market. You'll have to determine how much space will continue to be available, how your space compares to the rest of the marketplace and determine how quickly the space will be leased.

You must also consider the implications of current economic factors that might increase or decrease the vacancy rate in the area. Complex analysis of these factors is beyond the scope of this text. However, if a lot of inventory is under construction currently and the economy is slowing down, you should adjust your absorption calculation down.

## Summary

Gathering data and analyzing it is a critical component of your job when working for your buyers and sellers. For buyers, we must determine what the property may be worth, what the highest and best use of the property may be, and how we might improve the property. For sellers, we must also examine the value of the property, the highest and best use and any improvements that may increase our ability to obtain a higher price and better terms.

Research falls into different categories. In order to understand the property, we must gather all the information we can about the specific property, including income and expense data, building and property size, and all physical information about the building and property. We must also research the zoning and potential uses of the property.

Research is not limited directly to the property, either. We need to analyze the economic and demographic data of the surrounding area and surrounding properties to understand the market and the impact of selling or leasing the property in the current economic climate. We must also check the availability of financing.

Last, we need to compare the property with similar properties on the market to determine where the property fits with the competition, and review properties that have recently sold to determine what buyers or tenants are paying for similar properties.

# Chapter 2: Review Questions

1.  Zoning regulations may include all of the following except:

    A. Setback requirements
    B. Maximum height restrictions
    C. Maximum site coverage
    D. Parking restrictions
    E. All are common zoning restrictions

2.  Property Data Gathering and Research includes all the following except:

    A. Income Data and Analysis
    B. Direct Comparison with other properties
    C. Economic Data on the surrounding area
    D. Data on the property's current financing
    E. Zoning Data and potential uses

3.  Office Vacancy Rates are calculated by:

    A.  Number of Units Leased divided by the Total Number of Units
    B.  Number of Vacant Units divided by the Total Number of Units
    C.  Occupied Square Footage divided by Total Square Footage
    D.  Vacant Square Footage divided by Gross Leaseable Square Footage
    E.  Vacant Square Footage divided by Total Square Footage

4.  Local Vacancy Rates can be affected by all the following except:

    A. National Economy
    B. Competing New Construction
    C. Anti Construction Sentiment
    D. Financing Interest Rates
    E. All choices can affect local vacancy rate

5.  True or False: Setbacks are commonly equal along all lot lines including front, rear and sides.

6.  If the total square footage of vacant retail space on the market in your area in January of last year was 452,000 square feet, and January 1st of this year, that number was

460,000 square feet, but 200,000 square feet of space was constructed during the year, what is the monthly absorption rate of the market?

7. True or False: Area lifestyle and colleges do not affect property value.

8. If a lot contains 1.2 acres, and zoning restricts the maximum impervious surface sit coverage to 40%, and the maximum building size to 25%, what is the maximum building size and maximum impervious surface area?

9. For a new 5000 square foot office building, zoning requires 4 parking spaces per 1000 square feet. Each parking space must be a minimum of 10' x 20' with a 20' back out area. What is the minimum square footage the parking lot will cover?

10. List 2 potential environmental issues with industrial properties.

11. Calculate the vacancy rate of a 5 unit multifamily property for the past year. 3 of the units were vacant for 1 month each, and 1 unit was vacant for 2 months during the past year.

# 3

# Investment Analysis

All commercial real estate is an investment. Although some buyers and tenants are users of the property and others are investors, both consider the property to be an investment. A property user purchases or leases commercial real estate in order to have a place to conduct or house their business. The user's return might be directly from their business, or their return on their investment in a property may be a combination of what they receive in appreciation in their equity in the property and what they receive as a return on their business assets. Straight investors, who do not occupy the property, purchase property in order to realize a return on their investment in the property. Part of that return is captured in cash flow, and part of that return is appreciation and equity build-up and is ultimately realized when the property is eventually sold. You will also meet clients who are a combination of user and investor who will purchase more real estate than needed for their business in order to obtain a return above and beyond their personal business.

Certainly, whole courses exist on Real Estate Investment Analysis. Our goal in this chapter is to introduce you to the concept of income and cash flows, the primary methods of calculating return on investment, and how they are important to the marketing and sale of commercial real estate. We will outline the various forms of calculating returns on investment, but an in-depth analysis of income projection is beyond the scope of this text.

## The Benefits to Owning Investment Real Estate

An important part of understanding investment real estate is determining why individuals and corporations purchase real estate. Some of the primary reasons include:

1.  **Increase in Overall Investment Value (Appreciation)** - Over the long term, investing in real estate has consistently been proven one of the best vehicles for investment returns. Commercial and Investment real estate can appreciate, or grow in value, even when the economy is declining, or when other investments are declining or unstable. If property values continue to rise and the investor continues to pay the mortgage, the investor's equity will steadily increase.

2.  **Investment Growth Without Additional Capital** – Typically, investors do not have to invest money month after month or year after year in the same property, as they would in a 401K or other retirement program. The investor or owner of the property is building equity in the property by making payments on a mortgage that is generally paid by tenants or income derived from the property. Any repairs or maintenance can be covered by the rental income.

3.  **Tax Benefits** - Investing in Real Property can also offer substantial tax benefits not found in many other investments. Tax benefits can include write offs, as well as "depreciation" that can offset your income. Tax benefits may vary from area to area, and from investor to investor based on an investor's holdings. An owner or investor should always seek advice and information from an expert accountant and attorney.

4.  **A Leveraged Investment** - Purchasing Real Estate as an investment enables an investor to maximize his or her investing power through leverage. Using leverage, an average real estate investor can secure hundreds of thousands or millions of dollars in real estate by investing only a fraction of the actual cost. The balance is provided by a lending institution or private lender.

5.  **Substantial Returns** – In addition to income from property rental and tax benefits, the property may appreciate in value over time. As the property appreciates, the owner receives the full benefit of the increase in value. For example, an investor purchases a $250,000 property with a 10% down payment and closing costs, or $25,000. If the property appreciates at a rate of 3% per year, that is 3% of the full property value of $250,000. In 1 year, the property has appreciated by $7500, or 3% of $250,000. This $7500, however, is a return of 30% on the buyer's initial investment of $25,000.

## Types of Real Estate Investors:

Potential investors and commercial property buyers fit every walk of life. Some are business people in suits or heads of corporations, groups of doctors or the auto mechanic at the end of the street. Investors in commercial property are more often defined by their ultimate goals. Investor types include:

1.  **Speculators** – These are Investors who buy real estate at low prices, hoping that an increase in value will warrant their purchase and they'll make money. Their mantra is to buy low and sell high. Speculators often buy land parcels or properties in high growth markets where the property appreciation rate will hopefully outpace other forms of investment returns.

2.  **Flippers** – are Investors who want to buy real property at a low price, renovate or "fix up" the property and re-sell at a higher price. In commercial real estate, a flipper may be a buyer who purchases a property in order to alter the use of the property to a higher use, or sell the property and the components of the property (cranes, equipment) back off separately for a higher total price.

3.  **Income Stream Investors** – are Investors who buy real estate to rent the properties to tenants, earn a return on their investment over time and re-sell the property at some point in the future.

4.  **Users or End-Users** – Individuals who buy investment or commercial property for their business. Ray Kroc, founder of McDonalds Corporation, was in the real estate business. The sale of hamburgers and fries funded his real estate acquisitions.

5.  **Developers** – Investors or groups who purchase property in order to utilize or prepare the site for a different use. Developers often purchase raw land and subdivide the land into smaller increments to be sold. Developers may take raw land or underutilized land and develop it for a higher use.

Investors may be:

1.  **Individuals or families**.

2.  **Partnership Investment Pools**- Investors who join with other investors to purchase properties or businesses that provide an income stream. These include Tenants in Common pools or TICs.

3.  **Corporate Investors**- Insurance companies, Real Estate Investment Trusts and others.

# Understanding Investment Income

Any commercial property that can be leased can generate a revenue stream to the owner. Income on the property can come from rent from tenants, or from other income such as laundries, billboards, and soda machines. Income is generally described as Scheduled Gross Income, Effective Gross Income, Gross Income, Net Income or Net Cash Flow. It is important to understand what each term means.

**Scheduled Gross Income**

Scheduled Gross Income is the total income a property *could* generate if all units were rented. This number is computed by adding the rents from all occupied units and adding the market rent for any un-rented units. Although Scheduled Gross Income could refer to monthly income, it is generally used to describe yearly income, so the rent is then multiplied by 12 months.

> Sum of All Rents x 12 months
> + Market Estimate of Rent for any unoccupied units x 12 months
> - - - - - - - - - - - - - - - - - - - - - - - - - - - - - - - - - -
> = Scheduled Gross Income

---

**Example**: An office building contains 6 units. 5 units are occupied with 1 unit vacant. The occupied units currently rent for $900, $1000, $750, $1250 and $1100 per month. The vacant unit has a market rent of $1000 per month. What is the Scheduled Gross income?

Step 1: Sum All Rents
$900 + $1000 + $750 + 1250 + $1100 = $5000 per month

Step 2: Sum all vacant units at market rents
1 unit x $1000 per month = $1000 per month

Step 3: Add Rents and Vacant Unit Estimates
$5000 + $1000 = $6000

Step 4: Multiply by 12 months to obtain a yearly figure
$6000 x 12 = $72,000

Scheduled Gross Income = $72,000

---

**Effective Gross Income (EGI)**

Effective Gross Income is the total income a property could generate if all units were rented less a factor for vacancy. Calculate the average of the past 3 years vacancy rates, if the rates are available, and subtract that number from the Scheduled Gross Income. This method will give a more accurate picture of how much an investor can expect to gross on the property.

> Sum of All Rents x 12 months
> \+ Market Estimate of Rent for any unoccupied units x 12 months
> \- Vacancy Factor
> \- - - - - - - - - - - - - - - - - - - - - - - - - - - - - - - - - - - - - -
> \= Effective Gross Income

---

**Example:** The office building in the above example had a vacancy rate over the last 3 years of 3%, 7% and 5%, respectively. What is the Effective Gross Income?

Step 1: Average the vacancy rate of the last 3 years
(3% + 7% + 5%) / 3 Years = 5% per year

Step 2: Multiply Scheduled Gross Income by Vacancy Rate
$72,000 x 5% = $3600

Step 3: Subtract the Vacancy Rate from the Scheduled Gross Income
$72,000 - $3600 = $68,400

Effective Gross Income = $72,000

---

**Gross Income (GI)**

Unfortunately, different commercial and investment agents use the term Gross Income to refer to either Scheduled Gross Income or Effective Gross Income. In this text, we shall define Gross Income to be the Effective Gross Income after a vacancy factor has been subtracted from the Scheduled Gross Income.

**Net Operating Income (NOI)**

Net Operating Income or Net Income is the remaining income after all operating expenses have been paid. Operating expenses, which will be examined in the next section, include property taxes, insurance, utilities, maintenance and management. Operating expenses do not include the principal and interest of the mortgage payment.

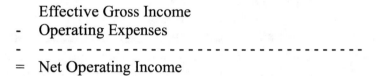

```
    Effective Gross Income
-   Operating Expenses
-   - - - - - - - - - - - - - - - - - - - - - - - - - - - - - - - - - - -
=   Net Operating Income
```

**Net Cash Flow**

The Net Cash Flow is the cash remaining after the mortgage payment is deducted from Net Operating Income. The Net Cash Flow can be further broken down into a figure before income taxes are taken out of the Cash Flow and after taxes are taken out.

- Cash Flow Before Taxes (CFBT)- Simply the Net Operating Income (NOI) less an owner's yearly principal and interest mortgage payment, also called their Annual Debt Service.

```
    Net Operating Income
-   Annual Debt Service (Mortgage Principal & Interest)
-   - - - - - - - - - - - - - - - - - - - - - - - - - - - - - - - - - -
=   Cash Flow Before Taxes
```

- Cash Flow After Taxes (CFAT) – An owner's actual cash flow after paying income tax on the Cash Flow.

```
    Cash Flow Before Taxes
-   Tax Liability
-   - - - - - - - - - - - - - - - - - - - - - - - - - - - - - - - - - -
=   Cash Flow After Taxes
```

# Understanding Operating Expenses

Operating Expenses are those expenses that must be paid by the owner to operate and maintain the property. Operating Expenses include property taxes, property insurance, utilities paid by the owner, maintenance and management. These expenses do not include the principal and interest of the mortgage payment.

These expenses do not include any tenant paid expenses, simply because they are not paid by the owner. In the example of a 6 unit office building, if the electric is separated to the individual units and the tenants are paying for that electric usage, that utility cost is *not* part of the operating expenses. However, if there is a common hallway, common bathrooms and an elevator, the owner or landlord should have a separate electric meter and *those* electric utility costs *are* part of the operating expense.

When selling retail or office properties, tenants often pay Common Area Maintenance (CAM) Fees, which help to cover the expenses paid by the owner of the property. If these expenses are reimbursed by the tenants as CAM fees, they either are not part of the operating expenses, or the CAM fees are added back into the Scheduled Gross Income.

Operating Expenses must be accurately determined or estimated in order to accurately price a property for a seller or assist a buyer in determining the property's investment return. These expenses fall into two categories: fixed expenses and variable expenses.

## Fixed Expenses

Fixed expenses are those expenses that do not change regardless of whether or not the property is occupied. Whether correct or incorrect, most real estate agents also include expenses that will not fluctuate during a one year period.

Property taxes and property insurance are considered fixed expenses. These are expenses that may fluctuate from year to year, but generally remain stable for the entire year, and the owner will pay those expenses whether or not the property is occupied. Other expenses that may be fixed are refuse, security and pest control.

## Variable Expenses

Any expenses paid by the owner or landlord that will increase or decrease depending on the occupancy of the property are variable expenses. Typically these expenses also fluctuate from month to month. Utility expenses such as electric, heat, gas, water, and sewer are all typically variable expenses. Contracted services such as property management, snow removal, lawn care and cleaning may also be variable expenses.

## Reserves

At some point in time, the roof will have to be replaced, the parking lot repaved, the central air unit replaced and the bathrooms updated in the property you are selling. In order to fully account for any expenses that will be incurred in the future, a reserve fund should be set up by the owner or landlord. As you are calculating the cost of operating the property, a yearly reserve toward maintenance, repairs and updates should be included as part of the expenses.

When estimating the true and correct Net Income, after Operating Expenses, many real estate professionals neglect to include an amount for reserves toward building maintenance, repairs and updates. This is because the listing agent wants to show the "Return on Investment" to be the highest number possible in order to attract potential buyers.

On the other side of the transaction, a buyer's agent will be likely to estimate a reserve number that is high, when attempting to negotiate an offer on the buyer's behalf. The buyer's agent will want to show the property owner that the property may not be worth quite as much as he or she wants.

# Return on Investment

A client who is considering purchasing a commercial property will always want to know the current value of the property, the future value of the property at the time they plan to sell, and what kind of return they will receive for their investment in real estate rather than the stock market or the bond market. There are many valuation concepts that have relevance for different reasons.

Return on Investment is a performance metric to compare the income or return of an investment to another investment's return or to the expected return of the investor. The definition of Return on Investment is:

$$Return = \frac{(Gain\ from\ Investment - Cost\ of\ Investment)}{Cost\ of\ Investment}$$

In simplest form, a buyer or an investor wants to know what kind of return they can expect to receive by investing their money into a particular property. Although Real Estate can deliver some of the best returns available as an investment, and although it is an excellent tax shelter for an investor's income, it is a less liquid investment than a money market or mutual fund. Investors want assurances that the return will be worthy of the time and risk of their capital.

First, we have to determine what the client is actually investing in the property in order to compute the return on that investment. The investment is the down payment on the property plus the closing costs and any other ancillary costs paid by the buyer or investor in order to secure ownership of the property. Although there are circumstances where investors pay additional sums in property losses the first few years of ownership, we will assume in this text that all investors purchase properties that immediately have a positive cash flow.

To calculate the client's investment in the property, you can use the following formula:

```
     Purchase Price
  -  Mortgage Amount
  +  Buyer's Closing Costs or other Acquisition Costs
  - - - - - - - - - - - - - - - - - - - - - - - - - - - - -
  =  Initial Investment
```

Once you understand what the client is investing in the property, you can begin to calculate the return on that investment. There are several ways that Realtors evaluate the property's return:

- Cap Rate- or Capitalization Rate is a simple formula used by Commercial Real Estate Agents to obtain a rate of return on a buyer's money if the buyer were paying all cash for the property. It's a simple calculation of the Net Income of the property divided by the Sales Price.

$$\text{Cap Rate} = \frac{\text{Net Operating Income}}{\text{Sales Price}}$$

- Cash Flow Model- A projection of returns over the period of ownership of the property based on the initial investment in the property. This is a more complex calculation, but it's also more complete than a simple Cap Rate. The Cash Flow Model takes into account the actual investment made by the buyer, and the principal and interest payments of the buyer. Cash Flow can be projected in a spreadsheet or on a "T-bar" as we'll discuss later in this chapter.

- Net Present Value – The Present Value of the Future Benefits an investor will receive. Also known as Discounting, a Present Value calculation is a technique used to convert dollar amounts to be received in the future into a single 'Present

Value'. Discounting of cash flows is the direct opposite of compounding. Rather than place funds in an interest bearing account, or a compounding investment, the investor is foregoing the use of the funds in lieu of a perceived future benefit.

o     Internal Rate of Return- The inverse of Net Present Value. The rate of return that would make the present value of all the estimated future cash flows plus the final market value of the investment property or business opportunity equal to the current market price of the investment or opportunity. Or at what discount rate would create a Net Present Value of zero? This is a difficult concept for many Realtors to understand. There will be a more detailed look and examples later in this chapter.

# Cap Rate

Capitalization Rate or Direct Capitalization Rate, as described earlier, is a simple formula calculated by dividing the Net Income of the property by the Sales Price.

$$\text{Cap Rate} = \frac{\text{Net Operating Income}}{\text{Sales Price}}$$

Or

Net Income = Sales Price x Cap Rate

This formula is based on the general investment calculation of I-R-V:

Income = Interest Rate times Value

$$I = R \times V$$

$$\text{Rate} = \frac{\text{Value}}{\text{Income}}$$

This formula can be altered to assist a buyer is computing what they would deem to be a reasonable price for a particular property in a particular geographic area. The benefit to using Cap Rate as a measure of the value of a property is that it is easily calculated and accounts for the operating expenses of the property. It is also an easy way to compare the property with other properties in the same marketplace.

The problem with using this calculation as a rate of return on the property is that it is based on a single year net income and doesn't account for market conditions, property appreciation or depreciation, the buyer's mortgage interest rate or tax structure, and many other factors. Because property appreciation is not factored into this calculation, the formula is only useful in comparing properties in the same geographic area and circumstances.

---

**Example**: John Smith would like to buy a property with a 10% Cap Rate, and would also like to change his name to something more memorable. The Net Income on the property he's considering is $89,000. What is the maximum he would be willing to pay?

Answer:       Simply divide the Net Income by the Required Cap Rate

IRV:  Value = Income / Rate
Cap Rate Formula:  Price = Net Income / Cap Rate

$89,000 / 10% = **$890,000** Maximum Offer Price

---

# Understanding Cash Flows

Property Cash flow is income from a property. All future cash flows are estimated, because we do not truly know what the exactly what rental rates will be in the future, we don't know how much the property will appreciate or depreciate over any given period, and although we can estimate it, we don't know what the occupancy rate will be. A good realtor can forecast the income or the cash flow based on past performance.

There are two types of cash flows from a real estate investment:

- Annual Cash Flows – the cash flow generated by annual operation of a commercial property, or annual rental or income from the investment or commercial property.

- Property Sale Cash Flow – the cash flow generated by the sale of the property at some future point in time. This is also called reversion.

Hopefully, an investor will make money during the period of ownership through the leasing of the property or their personal use, which is the Annual Cash Flows. The property will hopefully appreciate in value over the period of ownership. Additionally, if the buyer or investor takes out a mortgage on the property when they purchase it, they will hopefully pay down the mortgage during that term of ownership. At the time the property is sold, the investor will realize the Property Sale Cash Flow.

To truly understand the return on the investment made by the buyer, they must take both cash flows into consideration.

Although many great programs exist to forecast the returns and cash flow of investment real estate, I think its critical to understand how forecasting is done. You can calculate cash flows by creating a simple spreadsheet in Excel, Lotus or Quattro Pro.

# Calculating Annual Cash Flows

In order to predict the investor's return, an outline of the income must be computed. You'll start with a first year's cash flow and then estimate increases in rent or expenses to compute each additional year in the schedule.

- Initial Investment- As shown earlier in the chapter, this can be defined either as the Down Payment plus Closing Costs or the Purchase Price plus Closing Costs less any Mortgages.

        Purchase Price
  -   Mortgage Amount
  +   Buyer's Closing Costs or other Acquisition Costs
  - - - - - - -   - - - - - - - - - - - - - - - - - - - - - - - - - - - -
  =   Initial Investment

- Effective Gross Income (EGI) - Because we don't truly know what the vacancy rate will be, we take the current gross rental income plus an estimate of the market rent for any vacant units (as if the property is 100% occupied) and deduct a vacancy rate.

        Scheduled Gross Rental Income (Monthly Rental Rate x 12)
  +   Other Income (from laundry, soda machines, etc)
  -   Vacancy Rate and Credit Losses
  -  - - - - - - - - - - - - - - - - - - - - - - - - - - - - - - - - -
  =   Effective Gross Income / Effective Rental Income

- <u>Net Operating Income (NOI)</u> – The difference between the Effective Gross Income and the Operating Expenses.

  Effective Gross Income
  - Operating Expenses
  - - - - - - - - - - - - - - - - - - - - - - - - - - - - - - - - - - - - -
  = Net Operating Income

## Accounting for Taxes

- <u>Cash Flow Before Taxes (CFBT)</u>- Simply the Net Operating Income (NOI) less an owner's yearly principal and interest mortgage payment, also called their Annual Debt Service)

  Net Operating Income
  - Annual Debt Service (Mortgage Principal & Interest)
  - - - - - - - - - - - - - - - - - - - - - - - - - - - - - - - - - -
  = Cash Flow Before Taxes

  > **Example**: Property maintains a Net Operating Income of $25,000, and the investor's principal & interest mortgage payment will be $1000 per month or $12,000 per year:
  >
  >    $25,000  (NOI)
  > -  $12,000   (Mortgage P&I)
  > -  - - - - - - - - - - - - - - - - -
  > =  $13,000   (Cash Flow Before Taxes)

- <u>Tax Liability</u>- Income taxes are paid on the Cash Flow less the Interest paid, less any depreciation of the property. Properties may be depreciated on an owner's taxes to reduce their tax liability. Calculations for depreciation are beyond the scope of this text.

  Cash Flow Before Taxes
  - Mortgage Interest Paid
  - Property Depreciation
  - - - - - - - - - - - - - - - - - - - - - - - - - - - - - - - - - - - -
  = Tax Liability

Property Depreciation is calculated based on the type of property and the time the investor has owned the property. Appendix A outlines some of the conditions of depreciation.

- Cash Flow After Taxes (CFAT) – An owner's actual cash flow after paying income tax on the Cash Flow.

    Cash Flow Before Taxes
    - Tax Liability
    - - - - - - - - - - - - - - - - - - - - - - - - - - - - - - - - - - - -
    = Cash Flow After Taxes

## Complete Cash Flow Calculation

- Complete Annual Cash Flow Calculation- Additionally, to get a true picture of the cash flow generated to the property's owner, we put the entire equation together:

    Scheduled Gross Rental Income
    + Other Income
    - Vacancy Rate & Credit Losses
    - - - - - - - - - - - - - - - - - - - - - - - - - - - - - - - - - - - -
    = Effective Gross Income (EGI)
    - Operating Expenses (OE)
    - - - - - - - - - - - - - - - - - - - - - - - - - - - - - - - - - - - -
    = Net Operating Income (NOI)
    - Annual Debt Service (Mortgage Principal & Interest)
    - - - - - - - - - - - - - - - - - - - - - - - - - - - - - - - - - - - -
    = Cash Flow Before Taxes
    - Tax Liability
    - - - - - - - - - - - - - - - - - - - - - - - - - - - - - - - - - - - -
    = Cash Flow After Taxes

> **Example:**
>
> John Ruddsmucker has decided to make a bid on a 12 unit apartment building. Each unit is currently rented at $600 per month. There is no additional income for the property. The estimated vacancy rate is 5%, and operating expenses have been determined to be $12,080 per year. John's total initial investment (including down payment and closing costs) is $200,000, and he would finance $500,000 on a 20 year loan at 7% interest rate. John is in a 35% tax bracket. The answer is worked out on the following page:

**Cash Flow Calculation**

| | |
|---|---|
| Scheduled Gross Income (12 units x $600 x 12 months) | $86,400.00 |
| Less Vacancy Rate (5%) | -$4,320.00 |
| Effective Gross Income (EGI) | $82,080.00 |
| Less Operating Expenses (OE) | -$12,080.00 |
| Net Operating Income (NOI) | $70,000.00 |
| Less Annual Debt Service | -$46,518.00 |
| Cash Flow Before Taxes | $23,482.00 |
| Less Tax Liability* | $13,715.80 |
| Cash Flow After Taxes | $37,197.80 |

**\*Tax Liability**

| | |
|---|---|
| Cash Flow Before Taxes | $23,482.00 |
| Less Interest Paid | -$40,410.00 |
| Less Depreciation | -$22,260.00 |
| Tax Liability | -$39,188.00 |
| **Taxes Saved (at 35%)** | **$13,715.80** |

# Calculating Property Sale Cash Flow

Property Sale Cash Flow is the cash received when the property is sold. This is the second type of return on investment received by the owner. The net proceeds are also termed Reversion Cash Flow.

```
    Sales Price
 -  Initial Investment (Down Payment + Closing Costs)
 -  Mortgage Balance
 -  - - - - - - - - - - - - - - - - - - - - - - - - - -
 =  Net Proceeds Before Taxes
 -  Capital Gains Taxes
 -  - - - - - - - - - - - - - - - - - - - - - - - - - -
 =  Net Proceeds After Taxes
```

**Reversion** is the term used by Real Estate practitioners to describe the lump sum benefit an investor expects at the sale of a property.

# Multi Year Cash Flow Forecasts

In order to understand the true return on your client's initial investment, you'll need to compute the cash flow from the entire holding period for the property. A buyer may have a pre-determined period of time he or she would like to own the property. Each year of this expected holding period, the property generates an Annual Cash Flow. At the end of the anticipated ownership period, the property generates a Property Sale Cash Flow. In order to appropriately determine the benefits derived from the Cash Flows, they'll need to be "discounted" back to the Present Value. That will be discussed in the next section.

Unless the property is located in a high appreciation location, an investor or investors must hold onto the property for several years in order to recapture the costs they've incurred in closing costs to purchase the property and to sell the property. A typical holding period for many commercial investors is 5 to 7 years.

## Multi Year Forecasts

First – Determine the buyer's holding period or ownership period.

Second – Complete a first year Cash Flow chart from available income and expense data.

Third - Estimate the income and expenses for each year of the holding period and calculate the Annual Cash Flow.

Fourth – Estimate the eventual sales price of the property in the final year in order to determine the Property Sale Cash Flow.

Five factors are necessary in order to create a Multi Year Cash Flow Forecast:

1.   The <u>Holding Period</u> must be identified or estimated.

2.   The <u>Initial Investment</u> must be known.

3.   The <u>Annual Cash Flow</u> for the current year must be calculated.

4.   The <u>Rate of Change of Income and Expenses</u> must be estimated.

5.   The <u>Sales Proceeds</u> must be estimated for the ultimate sale of the property.

Once you have a holding period and an initial investment figure identified, you'll need to complete a first year Annual Cash Flow statement. After completing the statement, you can begin estimating the income and expenses for each year of the holding period.

## Estimating Incomes and Expenses

Whether you are working with commercial property sellers to project the future growth or decline of a property, or working with potential buyers to predict the most likely sales price of the property at some point in the future, you'll have to estimate future incomes and expenses.

Unfortunately, there's no crystal ball that will tell you exactly what is going to happen in any particular type of property or any particular marketplace. You'll have to judge the likelihood of potential increases or decreases. When analyzing a property to buy or sell, first consider the following questions:

1.    Are the rents currently at market rent, or are they low or high for the market? Do you expect market rents to remain stable in the future? Are there any pending changes in zoning or employment locally that may affect market rents?

2.    Are competing properties in better condition or worse condition than the subject? Will the condition impact the rental of any vacant units? Does the subject need significant repairs which will impact the initial investment of the buyer in the property?

3.    Are there any areas of the property that are likely to need major repairs or renovations in the next few years, or during the holding period of the property?

4.    Are there any pending or anticipated assessments against the property, such as new sewer lines or new sidewalks in an area?

5.    Are there any major changes occurring in the neighborhood which could affect the property's value?

6.    Are any tax changes or significant utility changes expected which would affect the income stream from the property?

Once you have an understanding of the marketplace and the potential changes, you can begin to estimate the future income and expenses. Again, although there are brilliant statisticians in the world who make predictions regularly, there is no magic to estimating future income and expenses. You'll need to determine a realistic growth factor or appreciation for the income and expenses (or decline if you believe there will be decrease). One way to calculate an acceptable appreciation factor is to determine the increase in income and expenses over the prior 3 to 5 years and average those increases to find an appreciation factor. A deeper analysis of the market might be found by contacting local economic development organizations and appraisers to obtain their view of the likely increase in market rents and expenses.

Sellers often raise rental rates on their tenants shortly before selling the property, in order to show the property close to maximum potential income. Some real estate professionals consider the first two years of the holding period at a stable level, and then increase both income and expenses for the remaining years of the holding period to compensate for this factor.

Please review the first example on the next page. In that example, there are several assumptions that either the agent or the buyer is making about the property. First, the agent or buyer is assuming that the rent will continue to increase at 2% per year. This may be high, low or accurate. Secondly, the buyer is assuming that the property will sell at the end of year 5 for $850,000. This assumption is probably based on the buyer's estimation of appreciation.

However, although there are pockets throughout the country where investors purchase rental properties at losses because they expect appreciation, in most areas rental property prices tend to be based on their incomes. The current buyer is offering $750,000 for a Net Income of $71,680. This is a Cap Rate of 9.55%. At the end of year 5, the Net Income is $76,067. At a Cap Rate of 9.55%, that would indicate a value of $796,513, which is far short of the $850,000.

Another consideration is that the investor would not be selling the building based on the income from year 5, but rather year 6 when the new buyer takes possession. Even if the net income rises 2% to $77,588, with a Cap Rate of 9.55%, the value would be $812,439. The investor is assuming the buyer in 5 years will pay based on a lower Cap Rate than the current buyer.

If the buyer realizes the 2% increase in yearly rental income and the $850,000 sales price, the buyer will have earned a return on his initial investment of 9.55% the first two years, and a slightly higher return each additional year. At the end of the holding period, an additional return comes from selling the property. The total cash flow received over the 5 year holding period is $538,796.86 from an initial investment of $750,000.

In the second example on the following page, the investor only invests $150,000. The return from the Annual Cash Flow for the first year is 10.57%, higher than the un-leveraged model. The Total Cash Flow received over the 5 year holding period is $203,870.86, which is a yield of 135.9%, or 27.18% return per year. In both these examples, the actual returns will have to be discounted back to Present Value in order to accurately reflect the return on the investment, as we'll describe in the next section.

In the second case, leveraging the property by accepting a mortgage allows the buyer to earn money on the lender's investment in the property. In this case, the mortgage rate is 7%, and the investor is earning a spread on the income above the 7% payment.

<u>Example 1</u>: A buyer purchases an office building with an anticipated holding period of 5 years. The buyer pays all cash for the building. Current rental income for the 6 units is $6000 per month. Owner paid expenses include $5000 for yearly property taxes, $1500 for yearly owner paid electric, $1500 for property insurance, $800 for refuse and $1000 for water and sewer. Rents have increased an average of 2% per year for the last 3 years, and vacancy has averaged 3%. The buyer is purchasing the building for $750,000 and anticipates selling the building in 5 years for $850,000. Estimate the multi year income and expenses.

| Income and Expenses | Year 1 | Year 2 | Year 3 | Year 4 | Year 5 |
|---|---|---|---|---|---|
| **Income:** | | | | | |
| Scheduled Gross Income | $84,000.00 | $84,000.00 | $85,680.00 | $87,393.60 | $89,141.47 |
| Less Vacancy | -$2,520.00 | -$2,520.00 | -$2,570.40 | -$2,621.81 | -$2,674.24 |
| Effective Gross Income | $81,480.00 | $81,480.00 | $83,109.60 | $84,771.79 | $86,467.23 |
| | | | | | |
| **Operating Expenses:** | | | | | |
| Real Estate Taxes | $5,000.00 | $5,000.00 | $5,100.00 | $5,202.00 | $5,306.04 |
| Property Insurance | $1,500.00 | $1,500.00 | $1,530.00 | $1,560.60 | $1,591.81 |
| Liability Insurance | $0.00 | $0.00 | $0.00 | $0.00 | $0.00 |
| Utilities: Electric | $1,500.00 | $1,500.00 | $1,530.00 | $1,560.60 | $1,591.81 |
| Utilities: Heating | $0.00 | $0.00 | $0.00 | $0.00 | $0.00 |
| Utilities: Water / Sewer | $1,000.00 | $1,000.00 | $1,020.00 | $1,040.40 | $1,061.21 |
| Garbage / Refuse | $800.00 | $800.00 | $816.00 | $832.32 | $848.97 |
| Maintenance | $0.00 | $0.00 | $0.00 | $0.00 | $0.00 |
| Property Management | $0.00 | $0.00 | $0.00 | $0.00 | $0.00 |
| Professional Services | $0.00 | $0.00 | $0.00 | $0.00 | $0.00 |
| Security | $0.00 | $0.00 | $0.00 | $0.00 | $0.00 |
| **Total Operating Expenses** | $9,800.00 | $9,800.00 | $9,996.00 | $10,195.92 | $10,399.84 |
| | | | | | |
| **Net Operating Income** | $71,680.00 | $71,680.00 | $73,113.60 | $74,575.87 | $76,067.39 |
| | | | | | |
| Less Annual Debt Service (P&I) | $0.00 | $0.00 | $0.00 | $0.00 | $0.00 |
| **Cash Flow Before Taxes** | $71,680.00 | $71,680.00 | $73,113.60 | $74,575.87 | $76,067.39 |

| Yearly Cash Flow | Year 0 | Year 1 | Year 2 | Year 3 | Year 4 | Year 5 |
|---|---|---|---|---|---|---|
| Initial Investment | -$750,000.00 | | | | | |
| Yearly Cash Flow | | $71,680.00 | $71,680.00 | $73,113.60 | $74,575.87 | $76,067.39 |
| Prop Sale Cash Flow | | | | | | $850,000.00 |
| **Cash Flow Per Year** | ($678,320.00) | $71,680.00 | $71,680.00 | $73,113.60 | $74,575.87 | $926,067.39 |
| | | | | | | |
| Total Cash Flow | $538,796.86 | | | | | |

Example 2: Using the same example as the previous page, let's analyze the returns per year if the buyer leveraged the property. Rather than invest $750,000 in an all cash transaction, the buyer invests $150,000 and borrows $600,000 at 7% on a 20 year amortized loan.

| Income and Expenses | Year 1 | Year 2 | Year 3 | Year 4 | Year 5 |
|---|---|---|---|---|---|
| **Income:** | | | | | |
| Scheduled Gross Income | $84,000.00 | $84,000.00 | $85,680.00 | $87,393.60 | $89,141.47 |
| Less Vacancy | -$2,520.00 | -$2,520.00 | -$2,570.40 | -$2,621.81 | -$2,674.24 |
| Effective Gross Income | $81,480.00 | $81,480.00 | $83,109.60 | $84,771.79 | $86,467.23 |
| **Operating Expenses:** | | | | | |
| Real Estate Taxes | $5,000.00 | $5,000.00 | $5,100.00 | $5,202.00 | $5,306.04 |
| Property Insurance | $1,500.00 | $1,500.00 | $1,530.00 | $1,560.60 | $1,591.81 |
| Liability Insurance | $0.00 | $0.00 | $0.00 | $0.00 | $0.00 |
| Utilities: Electric | $1,500.00 | $1,500.00 | $1,530.00 | $1,560.60 | $1,591.81 |
| Utilities: Heating | $0.00 | $0.00 | $0.00 | $0.00 | $0.00 |
| Utilities: Water / Sewer | $1,000.00 | $1,000.00 | $1,020.00 | $1,040.40 | $1,061.21 |
| Garbage / Refuse | $800.00 | $800.00 | $816.00 | $832.32 | $848.97 |
| Maintenance | $0.00 | $0.00 | $0.00 | $0.00 | $0.00 |
| Property Management | $0.00 | $0.00 | $0.00 | $0.00 | $0.00 |
| Professional Services | $0.00 | $0.00 | $0.00 | $0.00 | $0.00 |
| Security | $0.00 | $0.00 | $0.00 | $0.00 | $0.00 |
| **Total Operating Expenses** | $9,800.00 | $9,800.00 | $9,996.00 | $10,195.92 | $10,399.84 |
| **Net Operating Income** | $71,680.00 | $71,680.00 | $73,113.60 | $74,575.87 | $76,067.39 |
| Less Annual Debt Service (P&I) | $55,821.00 | $55,821.00 | $55,821.00 | $55,821.00 | $55,821.00 |
| **Cash Flow Before Taxes** | **$15,859.00** | **$15,859.00** | **$17,292.60** | **$18,754.87** | **$20,246.39** |

| Yearly Cash Flow | Year 0 | Year 1 | Year 2 | Year 3 | Year 4 | Year 5 |
|---|---|---|---|---|---|---|
| Initial Investment | -$150,000.00 | | | | | |
| Yearly Cash Flow | $15,859.00 | $15,859.00 | $15,859.00 | $17,292.60 | $18,754.87 | $20,246.39 |
| Prop Sale Cash Flow | | | | | | $250,000.00 |
| **Cash Flow Per Year** | **($134,141.00)** | **$15,859.00** | **$15,859.00** | **$17,292.60** | **$18,754.87** | **$270,246.39** |
| Total Cash Flow | $203,870.86 | | | | | |

# Understanding Present Value

In our example under Multi Year Cash Flow, we examined a property and determined the returns to be between 71.8% over 5 years and 135.9% over 5 years. However, in a true analysis of one investment vehicle over another, we need to take into account the <u>time value of money</u>.

If you loan a friend $100 today, and the friend returns the $100 in 5 years, the money is worth less. Certainly, it's the same $100, but as the cost of living increases, what can be purchased with that $100 is not the same in 5 years as it is today. Additionally, you lose the use of the money for that 5 year period. If you had invested that $100 in a money market or savings account, you would have earned interest on the money. Worse, you're investment in that money market would have produced a compounding effect, where you would be paid interest on the interest you receive.

> **Compounding** is process by which you earn interest on your interest. Your money or savings earn interest, and the interest stays in the investment, earning interest on the prior interest.
>
> **Discounting** is the process of converting future returns or future income into a single Present Value. The investor is purchasing a future benefit.

Since real estate investors are investing in a property which will provide an income stream over a period of time in addition to the appreciated sales price of the property at some point in the future, we need to understand what the value of that income stream and eventual sales price are in today's dollars. This Present Value of the expected future benefits will allow us to compare the property, as an investment, to other investment vehicles.

## Discounted Cash Flows

Discounting the Cash Flow to its Present Value is termed <u>Yield Capitalization</u>. Unlike Direct Capitalization (Cap Rate), which is a snapshot in time of one year's return divided by the initial investment to determine a property's value, Yield Capitalization takes into account the timing of the Cash Flows as well as the ultimate return by the appreciation or depreciation of the property's value.

In the realm of real estate investments, each Cash Flow received, whether Annual Cash Flow from rental income or Property Sale Cash Flow, must be discounted back to a Present Value number based on the time and an assumed interest rate, called the Discount Rate, and then add them.

The **Discount Rate** can be the expected inflation rate, to analyze the current value of the Cash Flow while adjusting for inflation. If Net Present Value is being used to compare two different investments, the Discount Rate could be the expected rate of return on the alternate investment. If an investor believes they will receive a 5% return on an investment in a CD, you can compare the Net Present Value of the Cash Flow from a property to the CD by setting the Discount Rate in the Net Present Value calculation to 5%. If the Net Present Value of the property is positive, or greater than zero, then the return from the investment in the property will be greater than what an investor would have received from the 5% CD.

The Present Value of any individual Cash Flow is equal to the Future Value, or value received at the future date, multiplied by 1 plus the interest rate raised to the negative power of number of years. The formula for calculating the Present Value for any specific Cash Flow is:

$$PV = FV * (1 + i)^{-n}$$

Where PV = Present Value, FV = Future Value or Amount Received
i = expected interest rate per year, n = number of years

In order to calculate the Present Value of the series of Annual Cash Flows and Property Sale Cash Flow, each individual PV must be added

Example: If an investor is holding a property for 5 Years, 6 PV calculations must be performed and added together (5 Annual Cash Flows and 1 Property Sale Cash Flow).

Year 1: $PV1 = FV * (1 + i)^{-1}$
Year 2: $PV2 = FV * (1 + i)^{-2}$
Year 3: $PV3 = FV * (1 + i)^{-3}$
Year 4: $PV4 = FV * (1 + i)^{-4}$
Year 5: $PV5 = FV * (1 + i)^{-5} + PSCF * (1 + i)^{-5}$
(PSCF is the Property Sale Cash Flow)

$PV = PV1 + PV2 + PV3 + PV4 + PV5$

---

Negative Exponents: Remember that a negative exponent means you need to divide by that number of factors instead of multiplying.

For example: $X^{-5} = 1 / X^5$ or $(1 + i)^{-2} = 1 / (1 + i)^2$

---

## Calculating Net Present Value Using Excel

Create a table in Excel or a similar spreadsheet program. Create a column of the Cash Flows, include the Property Sale Cash Flow in the final year Cash Flow. In Excel, the formula is NPV(discount rate, cash flow value range) + initial investment.

In the Example below, our column of Cash Flows is column E. Year 0 (line 2) indicates the initial investment, and Year 5 (line 7) indicates the Annual Cash Flow in Year 5 plus the Property Sale Cash Flow.

**Example**:

|    | A | B | C | D | E |
|----|---|---|---|---|---|
| 1  |        | **Income** | **Expense** | **Debt Service** | **Cash Flow** |
| 2  | **Year 0** | $0.00 | $0.00 | $0.00 | -$150,000.00 |
| 3  | **Year 1** | $81,480.00 | $9,800.00 | $55,821.00 | $15,859.00 |
| 4  | **Year 2** | $81,480.00 | $9,800.00 | $55,821.00 | $15,859.00 |
| 5  | **Year 3** | $83,109.60 | $9,996.00 | $55,821.00 | $17,292.60 |
| 6  | **Year 4** | $84,771.79 | $10,195.92 | $55,821.00 | $18,754.87 |
| 7  | **Year 5** | $86,467.23 | $10,399.84 | $55,821.00 | $270,246.39 |
| 9  |        |   |   |   |   |
| 10 | **Interest Rate** | 3% |   |   |   |
| 11 | **NPV** | $145,951.26 |   |   |   |

In this case, the NPV (on line B-11) is the following formula:

$$= NPV(B10,E3:7) + E2$$

Key:  B10 = A Discount Rate of 3%
      E3:7 = The range of Cash Flows from Year 1 to Year 5
      E2 = The initial investment

The Net Present Value for this income is $145,951.26

# Internal Rate of Return (IRR)

The Internal Rate of Return is another method of comparing properties and comparing other investments by determining the yield on the investment. The definition of Internal Rate of Return is the Discount Rate that results in a Net Present Value of zero for a series of future Cash Flows.

In other words, to calculate the IRR, use a Net Present Value formula and set NPV to 0 and solve for the interest rate. This calculation is useful as a comparison between investments, but is, unfortunately, a difficult concept for both agents and investors to understand.

$$PV = 0 = FV * (1 + i)^{-n}$$

## Calculating Internal Rate of Return Using Excel

Create a table in Excel or a similar spreadsheet program. Just as with Net Present Value, create a column of the Cash Flows, include the Property Sale Cash Flow in the final year Cash Flow. Differing from Net Present Value, however, the first number in the column must be the initial investment. In Excel, the formula is IRR(cash flow value range).

In the Example below, our column of Cash Flows is column E. Year 0 (line 2) indicates the initial investment, and Year 5 (line 7) indicates the Annual Cash Flow in Year 5 plus the Property Sale Cash Flow. Unlike Net Present Value, we'll use all 6 lines in the calculation. IRR(E3:7).

| | A | B | C | D | E |
|---|---|---|---|---|---|
| 1 | | Income | Expense | Debt Service | Cash Flow |
| 2 | Year 0 | $0.00 | $0.00 | $0.00 | -$150,000.00 |
| 3 | Year 1 | $81,480.00 | $9,800.00 | $55,821.00 | $15,859.00 |
| 4 | Year 2 | $81,480.00 | $9,800.00 | $55,821.00 | $15,859.00 |
| 5 | Year 3 | $83,109.60 | $9,996.00 | $55,821.00 | $17,292.60 |
| 6 | Year 4 | $84,771.79 | $10,195.92 | $55,821.00 | $18,754.87 |
| 7 | Year 5 | $86,467.23 | $10,399.84 | $55,821.00 | $270,246.39 |
| 9 | | | | | |
| 10 | Interest Rate | 3% | | | |
| 11 | NPV | $145,951.26 | | | |
| 12 | IRR | 20% | | | |

The IRR (on line B-12) is the following formula:

$$= IRR(E2:7)$$

Key:    E2:7 = The range of Cash Flows from Year 1 to Year 5 including initial investment.

The Internal Rate of Return for this income stream is 20%

# Appraised Value VS Return on Investment

Realtors and Buyers are sometimes confused by the difference Appraised Value and Value based on the Return on Investment. Appraised value is not always what a buyer is willing to pay for a property. An appraisal is an estimate of value based on a combination of comparable sales, comparable rentals, the cost to reconstruct the property as well as the income of the property. Investors, on the other hand, are typically more interested in the potential income and potential return on their investment in the property.

## Appraised Value

If a prospective buyer of a commercial property requires a mortgage, the bank or lender will generally require an appraisal by a licensed Real Estate Appraiser. An appraisal is required by the lender in order to insure the lender that the property contains sufficient equity and value that the property could be re-sold to pay off the debt, should the buyer default on the loan.

The appraiser typically makes their determination of value by using several methods of comparison with other recently sold commercial or investment properties in the same general area and of the same type as the property being sold. In their final report to the lender, they will reconcile the three different approaches and give different weights to each. The primary three methods of comparison are:

- The market data approach – a comparison of the property to other properties of similar size, condition and use in the same area. Evaluating the property entails adjusting the value of the building by adding and subtracting for size, amenities and condition in comparison to other recently sold properties in the market.

- Reconstruction cost less depreciation – This approach determines value by determining the value of the land under the commercial building, and then adding the cost to rebuild the building at current market prices. The appraiser then subtracts the physical depreciation (wear, tear, and age) and any functional obsolescence (new buildings have features that older buildings do not). This is often a useful comparison if the building being purchased is relatively new, or to assist a buyer with comparison when considering purchasing an existing commercial building or constructing a new building.

- The income method – As part of an appraisal, this valuation method is still based on similar properties in the same area, but the comparison is strictly by the income generated by the property in comparison to the income generated by other similar properties recently sold in the market. If, for example, an appraiser finds that most properties are selling between ten and twelve times their Net Income, then the value of this commercial property probably lies in the same range.

Golf Courses are a specialized form of Hospitality Property and can be appraised by comparing them with other golf courses sold recently, unless the highest and best use of the property is something other than as a golf course.

# Putting the Numbers Together

## Evaluating and Price Investment Property

As we've discussed through this chapter, forecasting the return of an investment property is one of the primary responsibilities of a commercial real estate broker or agent. Whether your buyer is purchasing an office building to lease, a multifamily property to lease, or a shopping center, the buyer is looking for a stream of income that will provide a good return for the risk of his or her investment in the property.

Your first obligation when working with either a buyer or seller is to lay out a simple explanation of the income, the expenses and the possible returns. The form that I use is included on the next page.

## Property Information

Pur Price + Clos Cost _____ = Cash Invested _____
Mortgage:  Amount:  _____  Rate _____  P&I _____ x 12
                                                                            = _____
Depreciation (Res 27.5 yrs, Comm 39 yrs)  _____ x _____ % = _____

## Income & Expenses

Annual Rental Income _____ Less Vacancy _____ = Effective Gross Income _____
Annual Operating Expenses:
   Real Estate Tax _____ Insurance _____    Management _____
   Utilities _____   Repairs _____    Misc _____
Total Operating Expenses _____

## Calculations

Effective Gross Income                          _____
- Less Operating Expenses                   _____
= Equals Net Operating Income           _____
- Less Yearly Mortgage Payment (P&I)   _____
= Equals Cash Flow Before Taxes          _____

Annual Debt Service (Yearly P&I)          _____
- Less Interest                                        _____
= Principal Reduction                           _____

Net Operating Income                           _____
- Less Interest                                        _____
- Less Depreciation                               _____
= Equals Taxable Income                      _____
x multiplied by tax bracket                   _____
= Equals Taxes Paid or Saved               _____

## Rates of Return

Capitalization Rate = Net Op Income / Pur Price + Clos Cost  = _____ %

Cash on Cash Return = Cash Flow before Tax / Cash Invested = _____ %

Return = (CFBT + Principal Reduction +Taxes Saved) / Cash Invested = _____ %

# Chapter 3: Review Questions

1.  A buyer purchasing an investment property to house their personal business assets is:

    A.  An End-User
    B.  Developer
    C.  Flipper
    D.  Speculator
    E.  Income Stream Investor

2.  True or False: Speculators may buy properties that are losing money on rental income each month.

3.  Investors who purchase properties to fix up and resell are known as

    _____

4.  The acronym TIC stands for:

    A.  Tenant Investment Corporation
    B.  Tenants in Common
    C.  Transfer Income Conglomerate
    D.  Transaction Issuance Corporation
    E.  None of the Above

5.  The sum of all rents including estimates for vacant units is known as the:

    A.  Effective Gross Income
    B.  Scheduled Gross Income
    C.  Effective Rental Income
    D.  Net Income
    E.  Gross Rental Income

6.  An office building contains 4 units. 3 of them are currently rented at $1000, $1500 and $1200 respectively. The fourth unit is vacant, but has a market rent of $1000. Vacancy rates over the past 3 years have been 3%, 7% and 5%. Calculate the Effective Gross Income of the property.

7.    All of the following are fixed expenses except:

      A.    Property Taxes
      B.    Fire Insurance
      C.    Owner's Electric
      D.    Security

8.    True or False:  The term "reserves" refers to the money left over after paying taxes on an investment property.

9.    The formula for Cap Rate is _____.

10.   True or False:  Property Sale Cash Flow is also known as Reversion.

11.   Property appraisal uses all of the following techniques except:

      A.    Market Data Approach to Value
      B.    Reconstruction Cost Less Depreciation
      C.    Internal Rate of Return Calculation
      D.    Income Method / Income Comparison
      E.    All of the above are standard appraisal techniques

12.   True or False:  From an investor's perspective, the Discount Rate is the same as the opportunity cost.

# 4

# Commercial Leases

Leases are included in the Fundamental section of this text rather than the Practice section because leases are so integral to virtually every aspect of commercial real estate. A commercial agent or broker obviously must understand leases in order to lease and negotiate space for their clients, whether they are landlords or tenants. Additionally, leases and the various methods that building costs are split between landlords and tenants are an integral part of determining a property's value. The sales price of most income producing properties is directly related to the income the property or building generates after expenses. A full understanding of leases and how they function is necessary to properly advise your commercial investors and your property sellers.

## What is a Commercial Lease?

A lease is a legal contract designed to allow a person, group or entity to enjoy the use a property for a period of time in return for some compensation or value to the property owner, which is called typically called rent. Generally, a person or business leases an office, retail space or parcel of land and in return pays a monthly rental fee for the use of that property. Lease contracts are negotiated between the property owners, also known as landlords or **lessors**, and the property's end-users, also known as tenants or **lessees**. Commercial Realtors are often called upon to either represent the interest of the owner or landlord in procuring a tenant, and negotiating a lease with that tenant, or to represent a tenant or end-user to locate and acquire the lease of a property.

Lease contracts spell out the landlord and tenant names, the length of the contract, the amount of the lease payments, how the lease payment will be made, and who is responsible for maintenance and operation of the property. Lease contracts can also be negotiated to include almost any contingency that can be conceived. Some common contingency clauses include escalation of lease payments over time, first rights to purchase the property, the ability to sub-lease the property to another entity, and even a percentage of sales of the tenant.

Many end-users of commercial real estate prefer to lease space rather than purchasing. An end-user may lease because the location they desire is only available for lease, such as in a prominent shopping center, or a particular corner location. The user may lease because they don't have the capital to purchase a property, or they may have a strategy that will require them to move within a few years, and they'd rather not be tied to a particular building or location.

Owners or landlords often lease properties rather than selling them in order to obtain a Cash Flow from the property as a return on the investment they have in the property. Because commercial Realtors can represent either side of the transaction, it's important to understand the objectives and points of view of both landlords and tenants. In some objectives, landlords and tenants views are diametrically opposed from one another, and in other objectives, they are in perfect alignment.

## End-User or Tenants Objectives in Leasing Property

Although a tenant is willing to pay a fair market rent for a space that properly meets their needs, the user or tenant naturally wants to pay as little as possible to lease a property, and have the owner cover as much of the common area expenses as possible. Obviously a lower lease payment means more money in the tenant's pocket. A tenant is also looking for the right location, and a space that is suitable for their particular use. .

Other contingencies that benefit a tenant include:

- The Lease Payment will be locked into a particular payment for a long period of time.
- The Landlord will maintain the building or space.
- The Landlord will renovate the space to conform to the needs of the Tenant, or at least finance the renovation.
- The Tenant will have the right to sublet the space should the need arise.
- The Tenant will have the right to purchase the property at some future time.
- The Tenant will have the right to automatically renew the lease.

## Owner's or Landlord's Objectives in Leasing the Property

The owner of a property is generally looking for the highest rent payment in order to maximize the return on their investment in the property. Owners also desire tenants that will be stable, long term tenants, so that the owner doesn't have to search for a new tenant and re-rent the property. Additionally, owners seek tenants who will maintain the property and hopefully even improve the property over time at their own expense.

Other contingencies that benefit the landlord include:

- An escalation of the lease payment over time.
- The Tenant will maintain the building or space.
- The Tenant will make any improvements to the property, and all improvements are required to be approved by the Landlord.
- An Agreement that the Tenant will pay part or all of the variable costs of owning the building, including utilities and a percentage of maintenance, taxes and insurance.

## Points at which Tenants and Landlords Agree

Tenants and Landlords both desire the financial health of one another. If a Tenant is not financially solid, the Landlord may lose the tenant and have to re-rent the space, leaving it potentially vacant for a period of time. Or worse, a Landlord may have to evict a Tenant, losing time and money in the court system while trying to remove the Tenant from their property. Similarly, a Tenant desires a financially healthy Landlord because they don't want the negative impact of a foreclosure of the building or a lack of maintenance by the Landlord.

Other areas where Landlords and Tenants agree include having a clearly written lease that lays out exactly what the terms of the lease are, the amount of rent, what that rent includes, and the division of responsibilities for maintenance and utilities between the Landlord and Tenant.

# Types of Lease Payments

Leases are often defined by the type of payment negotiated between the Landlord and Tenant. If the Tenant pays a flat rate in a lease where the Landlord pays for all utilities and maintenance, the lease is called a Gross Lease. If the Tenant pays some part of the utilities, maintenance, taxes, insurance or operating expenses of the building or property, the lease is a Net Lease. The most commonly used terms for various lease payments include:

**Gross Lease** – Also known as a Full Service Lease, a Gross Lease is a lease in which the Tenant pays an all inclusive rental rate, meaning that the Landlord pays for all expenses to occupy, maintain and operate the building. These expenses paid by the Landlord include utilities (water, sewer, electric), property taxes, insurance, property maintenance (including snow removal and lawn care) and any common area expenses or security costs.

**Net Lease** – Although Net Leases often describe any lease where the Tenant pays all or some portion of the utilities and property operating expenses, the term is typically used by Realtors to refer to a lease where the Tenant pays the utilities such as water, sewer, electric and heat, and the Landlord pays all building expenses including taxes and insurance and the Tenant and Landlord separate the cost of maintenance of the property.

**Triple Net Lease** – The Tenant pays all expenses for the property with exception to capital improvements. Under a Triple Net Lease or Net-Net-Net Lease, the Tenant pays all utilities (electric, water, sewer, heat), property maintenance and the property taxes and insurance. If the Tenant is only leasing a portion of the property, the Landlord may pro-rate the cost of maintenance, taxes and insurance by the percentage leased by the Tenant. This is often done through the use of CAM, or Common Area Maintenance, fees.

**CAM Fees** – Common Area Maintenance Fees or Common Area Maintenance Assessments are a Tenant's prorated portion of all maintenance expenses of a property. In a Triple Net Lease, part or all of the cost of maintaining the building may be negotiated to the Tenant. This direct pass through of expenses from the Landlord to the Tenant allows the Landlord to receive a steady return on the property without concern about rising costs of maintaining the building.

**Percentage Lease** – A common type of lease found in malls and high end retail leases, a Percentage Lease requires the Tenant to pay a negotiated percentage of the Tenant's gross monthly or yearly sales made at the location in addition to a fixed minimum monthly rental payment.

**Hybrid Net Lease** – Any negotiated lease under which the Landlord and Tenant agree to share expenses of utilities, building maintenance or taxes and insurance between them.

| Gross Lease | Hybrid Net Lease | Net - Net - Net Lease |
|---|---|---|
| Landlord Pays Utilities<br>Landlord Pays Taxes, Insurance and Property Maintenance ↔ | Landlord Pays Some Expenses<br>Tenant Pays Some Expenses | ↔ Tenant Pays Utilities<br>Tenant Pays Taxes, Insurance and Property Maintenance |
| Landlord takes all risk for rising costs of utilities and maintenance | Some Shared Risk | Tenant takes all risk for rising costs of utilities and maintenance |
| ↔ | | ↔ |
| Lease Rate is High to cover Landlord's Expenses | Moderate Lease Rate | Lease Rate may be lower, but Tenant Pays all Expenses |

## Parts of a Commercial Lease

As you'll discover in your first few years in the Commercial Real Estate Industry, there are thousands of different leases. Although you'll find a great number of "standard" commercial leases available from Boards of Realtors and Real Estate Organizations, many leases are written by teams of attorneys at the request of individuals, groups or firms that own large properties in order to protect their interest. Some leases are written by attorneys as a negotiated agreement between Landlord and Tenant.

All leases have common elements that make them legal and binding. The lease must have the names of the parties, a description of the property being leased, and a rate of payment for the property. The most common elements are described below:

1. <u>Names of all parties</u> involved including owners / landlords and tenants / users. In most leases, the owner or landlord is referred to as the Lessor, and the tenant or user is referred to as the Lessee.

PRINCIPALS: This Agreement is between _____ hereinafter called Lessor, and _____ hereinafter called Lessee.

2. <u>Use of the property</u> / Legal objective of the tenant

> USE: Lessee shall occupy the premises only for the purpose of
> _____

3. <u>Proper Description of property</u> being leased.  This description should be complete and accurate.

> WITNESSETH:  Lessor agrees to let unto the Lessee premises being known as
> _____
> in the City / Township / Borough of _____, County of _____
> in the State of _____, Zip Code _____ with improvements consisting of
> _____

4. <u>Amount of Rent</u> and when payments must be made.

> Total rental for entire term payable to Lessor          $_____
> Payments shall be made in advance monthly for an amount of    $_____
> Due Date for each payment shall be _____
> Late Charge if rent is not paid within grace period of ____ days of Due Date $_____

5. <u>Start Date and End Date</u> of the lease.  The start date is the date the Tenant or Lessee begins paying for use of the property.  A Tenant may pay for the property prior to occupancy depending on what renovations they are making to the property.

> RENTAL TERM:
>     Start and End Date of Lease (also called "Term")
>     START DATE:  Lease Shall Commence on _____
>     END DATE: Lease Shall End on _____

6. <u>Written Form</u> – A commercial lease generally must be in a written form.

# Common Lease Clauses

There are literally hundreds of possible clauses that can be included in a lease. I've even seen lease clauses like "In the event of a nuclear war…" and "Should the property be completely destroyed by an act of God…" and dozens of other unique situations. A lease should spell out any "what if" situation that can occur during the term of the lease, and explain each party's responsibilities and restrictions. The most common and necessary clauses include:

1.  Property and Liability Insurance – Landlords will generally maintain a policy on the building, and Tenants will generally maintain a policy on their contents. A lease should spell out who is responsible for liability insurance and what each will cover.

2.  Property Improvements- Is the Tenant paying for improvements? Is the Landlord agreeing to pay for improvements? Will the Landlord pay for the improvements up front, and charge back the Tenant over time in the rent payment? Is the Tenant permitted to do renovations after they occupy the space? Must the tenant receive written permission from the Landlord for renovations or improvements?

3.  Repairs and Maintenance- Who is responsible? Are repairs differentiated between major repairs and maintenance for responsibility?

4.  Security Deposits- What is required? How will the deposit be returned?

5.  Common Area Maintenance Fees – and how they will be charged.

6.  Renewal Term – Will the lease automatically renew at the end of the lease? Will the lease convert to month-to-month until renegotiated?

7.  Lease Termination - Can either party cancel the lease prior to the expiration of the lease term? How much notice must be given by either party to cancel?

8.  Landlord's Right to Enter Property - Does the Landlord have the right to enter the property to do repairs or to check on his or her investment if reasonable notice is given to the tenants? What is the reasonable notice?

9.  Tenant Care of the Property – Explanation of how the property should be maintained under the lease.

10. Right to Sublease – Does the Tenant have the right to sublet the space?

11.    Remedies – What remedies do the Tenant and Landlord have if either breaches the contract?

# Term of a Lease

Lease terms vary from one month to ninety nine years depending on the needs of the Landlord and Tenants. Typical commercial leases, however, range between one and five years.   Tenants who prefer short lease terms may be concerned about their changing need for space over time.  However, short term leases may hurt a Tenant who may be replaced by a higher paying Tenant next year.  There is a cost for the Tenant to move an office or retail business from one location to another as well including relocating a phone system, furniture and simply the time involved in making a move.  Retail businesses may suffer when customers can't find them.

Long Term leases may be beneficial to either the Tenant or the Landlord depending on what the rate of increase for the rent payment might be.  If a Tenant locks in a specific rental rate for three to five years, the Landlord may suffer a paper loss if rental rates in the area rise significantly over the term of the lease.  Similarly, if overbuilding in an area leads to a reduction in rental rates, the Tenant may be locked into paying higher than typical rent in the area by a longer term lease.

# Quoting Rental Rates

Commercial rent is generally based the size of the property being leased.  The leasable area can vary depending on the type of property or the conventions of a particular area.  For example, office leasable area can include hallways or bathrooms.  You can obtain a complete set of standard rules for office space measurement from the Building Owners and Managers Association at www.BOMA.org.   In warehouse or industrial space, leasable area may include covered loading docks or the area in pole buildings on the property.

Rental rates are typically quotes as an annual figure.  For example, a lease rate of $16 per square foot for office space usually means $16 per square foot per year, or $1.25 per square foot per month.

In order to compute the tenant's monthly rent, the rate must be multiplied by the square footage of the leasable area and divided by 12 months:

**Example:**

Rent Per Year = $16 per Square Foot * 2625 Square Feet = $42,000

Rent Per Month = Rent Per Year ($42,000) / 12 Months = $3500

For tenants leasing a multiple use property, such as a property that is partially office space and partially warehouse space, the rate is generally blended between the two uses. Rather than quoting a rate of $16 per square foot for the office and $8 per square foot for the warehouse, the rental is quoted as a **blended rate** between the two uses.

## Landlord and Tenant Improvements

A common element in leases is the negotiation of improvements to the property being leased. Tenants will often want to reconfigure or improve the property to meet their business needs. Landlords may be willing to make capital improvements that will increase the overall value of the property, but will be unlikely to want to make specific improvements that would benefit only the specific tenant unless those improvements are included in the rental payment by amortizing the cost into the rental rate.

For this reason, properties leased with improvements specific to the tenant are often leased for longer periods of time, such as five to ten years, in order to incorporate the cost of the improvements.

Leases should also spell out whether or not the tenant is permitted to make improvements or renovations to the space without the landlord's written permission. Although tenant improvements will often improve the value of the property, there are renovations that are so specific to a particular tenant that it may devalue the property.

## Other Types of Leases

In addition to traditional leases, where a tenant or user leases a building or portion of a building for a period of time, there are alternative types of leases to suit almost any situation.

**Ground Lease** – Also known as a Land Lease, a Ground Lease is simply the lease of the land only. In a ground lease, a tenant or user will build their own structure on the property for their own business. Because of the nature of the cost involved to a tenant or user, these leases tend to be for very long periods of time, often more than ten years. Ownership of any building placed on the property reverts to the property owner at the end of the lease term. Users may be willing to lease the ground and build their own buildings or structures in a high traffic location because the user will generate a good return from their business on their investment into the property.

**Build-out Lease** – Also known as a built-to-suit lease. In a situation where the owner is willing to build-out a property to specifically suit the tenant, the cost of the construction is generally amortized into the lease of the space. For example, if an owner has a vacant lot and is willing to build a free standing building to suit the tenant's needs, the owner will want to increase the rent to compensate for the owner's additional construction cost. The same situation applies if a tenant is leasing a clear-span space in a warehouse or office building and wants the space finished into private offices.

**Sale and Lease-back** – This is a situation where the owner will sell the building to a buyer or investor, and lease back part or all of the building for their use. This happens in cases where the original owner still wants or needs use of the space, but may be property rich and cash poor. The owner wants or needs immediate capital while retaining use of the property. This can also occur when an owner no longer needs the entire space, or builds a building to suit the company needs, and would rather operate the business than be a landlord to other tenants in the building. Lease-backs are often long term net leases.

**Sub Lease** – A lease in which the original tenant of the property leases the space to someone else (or sublets the space). The original tenant is generally still responsible for the original terms of the lease to the landlord of the property.

**Assignment of Lease** – A tenant transfers all their interest in their current lease to a second party. Similar to a sublease, but the original tenant gives up their rights to occupy or lease the space. Responsibility for the leased property or the lease payments may only be released in an assignment with the written permission of the landlord or property owner.

# Chapter 4:  Review Questions

1.  The owner or landlord of a property is called the:

    A.  Lessor
    B.  Lessee
    C.  Operator
    D.  Assignee
    E.  Assignor

2.  True or False:  A Gross Lease is a lease in which the tenant pays for all utilities, but does not pay any percentage of the taxes.

3.  CAM fees are defined as: _____

4.  The Type of Lease in which a Tenant pays all expenses including utilities, insurance, taxes and maintenance is called:

    A.  Gross Lease
    B.  Net Lease
    C.  Hybrid Net Lease
    D.  Triple Net Lease
    E.  Percentage Lease

5.  An office building manager has agreed to rent your client a 1250 square foot office unit at $16.50 per square foot with CAM fees of $2.50.  What is the monthly cost for the new tenant to occupy the space?

6.  True or False:  A Lease-Back is a type of lease that allows the lessee to continue the lease from year to year without a written renewal until the landlord terminates the lease in writing.

7.  A Tenant transfers all their interest in their current lease to a second party, and with the landlord's permission, the original tenant gives up all rights to lease the space to the new tenant.  This is called:

    A.  Sub Leasing
    B.  Rental Transference
    C.  Lease Transference
    D.  Assignment of Lease
    E.  Lease Back

8.  The owner of a flex space building has agreed to complete a build-out of the inside of a space to turn 25% into offices. The entire space is 3000 square feet. The lease rate is $10, but the owner is charging an additional $2000 per month to cover his cost of improvements. There are no CAM fees on the building. What is the monthly cost to the tenant?

9.  True or False: Common Area Maintenance can include snow removal and lawn care.

10. Percentage Rent is generally found in what type of commercial property?

# 5

# Introduction to Commercial Mortgages

One of the great benefits of investing in Real Estate rather than other investments is the ability of the buyer or investor to leverage their investment by borrowing funds from a bank or other lending source. This ability to borrow funds allows an investor to make money on the spread between the earnings the investment property generates and the interest rate that the borrower pays the lender.

In order to fully comprehend both the benefits of property ownership, and the potential returns, you need to have a clear understanding of mortgages. First, a mortgage loan can be viewed as both a debt and an investment. The borrower considers the loan to be a debt against the property. The bank or lender views the loan as an investment that provides the bank with a return over time.

## Borrower's Perspective VS Lender's Perspective

The borrower usually wants to maximize the loan amount in order to leverage as much property as possible. The loan is viewed by the borrower as a debt that requires the borrower to make monthly payments for the next 20 or 25 years. The borrower's perspective is that he or she needs to make sure that the income from the property is higher than the loan payment. This spread between the income generated and the loan payment needs to be high enough that it provides the borrower with a good return on their initial investment.

The perspective of the lender is that the loan is an investment in the property and the borrower that will generate a return on the lender's money. The lender may loan a property buyer $200,000 on a $250,000 purchase at a fixed rate of 8% for a period of 20 years. The lender is making an investment in the property of $200,000, expecting a fixed annuity from this investment of 8% per year.

The lender will also be concerned about the borrower's ability to repay and the strength of the investment property to carry the mortgage loan. A lender will typically determine a purchase with a significant down payment to be less risky than a purchase with little or no down payment. Should the lender need to foreclose on the property, a significant down payment will hopefully insure the lender will be able to sell the property for enough to recapture their initial investment.

# Understanding Commercial Financing Terms

If you're planning to work as a commercial real estate agent or broker, you'll have to walk a line between passing financing questions to the lenders you work with, and giving information to your clients so you can show them that you know what you're talking about. The problem is that commercial loans and loan requirements change regularly, and vary from lender to lender. For example, you may find a lender with a private funding source who will loan 90% of the appraised value of a multifamily property with very few lender closing costs. Another lender across the street may loan a maximum of 80% of the appraised value and have very heavy fees.

The best scenario is to have a broad understanding of commercial lending, including the terms and methods of calculation, but let your clients know that for specifics, you'll need to confer with your lenders.

## Important Terms

- **Mortgage** – The Mortgage is the legal document that is filed at the local courthouse or recorders office that secures the property as collateral for the purchase of a property. This document secures the repayment of funds, because the lender may foreclose, or take back the property, if the loan is not repaid to the lender according to the terms of the mortgage.

- **Promissory Note** – The legal promise a borrower makes to the lender that they will repay the funds. This note accompanies the mortgage.

- **Loan to Value Ratio** - The ratio of the amount borrowed against a property to the appraised value of the property being secured by a mortgage. For example, a loan of $200,000 on an office building appraised at $250,000 would have a loan to value ratio of $200,000 / $250,000 or 80%. Loan to Value Ratio's are commonly referred to as LTV's.

- **Points** – Points refer to both prepaid interest on the borrowed funds, called discount points, and to origination fees paid to the lender as a fee for securing the mortgage, called origination points. A borrower can "buy down" an interest rate by prepaying some interest to the lender. A point is generally one percent of the mortgage amount. If a purchaser borrows $200,000, one point would be $2000.

- **Down Payment** – A buyer or investor will generally have to put some of their own money into the purchase of a property. Although there are times on particular properties with particular investors that a loan for 100% of the purchase price can be obtained, most purchases require a down payment. The down payment can be 10% of the purchase price, 20%, 30% or greater depending on the type of property, the strength of the borrower and the perceived risk to the lender. For example, taverns typically require a more substantial down payment than 4 unit apartment buildings because taverns have a much greater chance of failing and falling into foreclosure.

- **Closing Costs** – There are costs to purchase a property in addition to the down payment. These costs may be lender fees, such as points, or prepaid fees, such as prepaid property taxes, or pro-rated reimbursements. Closing costs will be discussed in more detail in the next section.

- **Mortgage Payment** – Mortgage loans are paid back to the lender over time. The Mortgage and Promissory Note outline the repayment terms. Mortgage payments are typically monthly, but some loans may be paid quarterly, bi-annually or annually.

- **Principal and Interest** – Each mortgage payment is made up partly of principal and partly of interest. The principal component is repayment of the loan balance. The interest payment is interest to the lender for the use of the principal.

- **Amortization** – Loans are typically repaid in equal monthly, quarterly or yearly installments. Each payment is made up partially of principal and partially of interest. Although the monthly payment does not change, in a fixed rate mortgage, the portion that is paid on principal increases over the life of the loan, and the portion that is paid in interest decreases.

- **Balloon Payment** – Many commercial loans are amortized over a long period of time, such as 15 or 20 years, but have a specific date when the balance of the loan is due and payable. For example, a loan may be amortized for 20 years, but require a balloon payment in 5 years for whatever balance is left on the loan at that point.

# Closing Costs

Closing costs can vary from area to area due to legal requirements and state or local fees. For example, in New Jersey, a buyer is required to have a survey of the property. In Pennsylvania, a buyer does not need a survey. In some states, a settlement must be conducted by a licensed Attorney. In Pennsylvania, a Title Agent will suffice to handle settlement. Fees can vary widely.

Even within a state, fees can change. In Lehigh County, where Allentown is located, there are transfer taxes of 2% of the purchase price split between buyer and seller. In Philadelphia, just south of Allentown, there is a 4% transfer tax split between the buyer and seller. The best method to learn about closing costs is to call a commercial lender in the area and ask them to meet with you and outline the potential fees.

The primary closing costs buyers may encounter are broken into four categories:

- **Lender Fees** – Any fees charged by the lender including origination points, discount points, appraisal, credit report, and preparation of mortgage documents.

- **Pre-paid Fees** – In many areas, property taxes must be paid at the beginning of a period, so you may pay property or school taxes at settlement. Other prepaid fees include property insurance and liability insurance.

- **Pro-Rations** – This concept is particularly important in any type of investment property. Typically, if property taxes or water and sewer fees are paid ahead, the buyer repays the seller for the unused portion. If the property is heated by oil or propane, a seller may require a buyer to pay the seller for the remaining fuel. In rental properties, whether the property is an office building, multifamily or other type of property, there may also be pro-rated rent or CAM fees. If all rents are paid on the first, and the property settles in the middle of the month, for example, the seller should pay the buyer half of the rental income for that month.

- **Other Closing Costs** – Title search or title insurance fees (which will be discussed in chapter 10), transfer taxes or sales taxes, any buyer brokerage fees, building inspector fees, recording fees for deeds or mortgages, notary fees, and surveys.

# Amortization

As explained above, loans are typically repaid in equal installments. Each payment is made up partially of principal and partially of interest. The exact amount of principal and interest each month can be calculated using a financial calculator, a mortgage software program, or one of the many public domain templates for Microsoft Excel.

On a fixed rate mortgage, the monthly payment does not change. However, the portion that is paid on principal increases, while the portion that is paid in interest decreases. The principal and interest payment is also known as the **debt service** of the property. This method of repayment insures that the bank receives more of their return early in the mortgage.

The spreadsheet below is for a $250,000 mortgage amortized over 20 years with an interest rate of 8%. The monthly payment is $2091.10, making the annual debt service a total of $25,093.20 (or $2091.10 multiplied by 12 months).

### Annual Amortization Schedule

| Year | Beginning Balance | Annual Payment | Annual Principal | Annual Interest | Cumulative Principal | Cumulative Interest | Ending Balance |
|---|---|---|---|---|---|---|---|
| 1 | $250,000 | $25,093.20 | $5,284.17 | $19,809.03 | $5,284.17 | $19,809.03 | $244,715.83 |
| 2 | $244,715.83 | $25,093.20 | $5,722.76 | $19,370.44 | $11,006.93 | $39,179.47 | $238,993.07 |
| 3 | $238,993.07 | $25,093.20 | $6,197.73 | $18,895.47 | $17,204.67 | $58,074.93 | $232,795.33 |
| 4 | $232,795.33 | $25,093.20 | $6,712.14 | $18,381.06 | $23,916.81 | $76,455.99 | $226,083.19 |
| 5 | $226,083.19 | $25,093.20 | $7,269.25 | $17,823.95 | $31,186.06 | $94,279.94 | $218,813.94 |
| 6 | $218,813.94 | $25,093.20 | $7,872.59 | $17,220.61 | $39,058.65 | $111,500.55 | $210,941.35 |
| 7 | $210,941.35 | $25,093.20 | $8,526.01 | $16,567.19 | $47,584.66 | $128,067.74 | $202,415.34 |
| 8 | $202,415.34 | $25,093.20 | $9,233.67 | $15,859.53 | $56,818.33 | $143,927.27 | $193,181.67 |
| 9 | $193,181.67 | $25,093.20 | $10,000.06 | $15,093.14 | $66,818.38 | $159,020.42 | $183,181.62 |
| 10 | $183,181.62 | $25,093.20 | $10,830.06 | $14,263.14 | $77,648.44 | $173,283.56 | $172,351.56 |
| 11 | $172,351.56 | $25,093.20 | $11,728.95 | $13,364.25 | $89,377.39 | $186,647.81 | $160,622.61 |
| 12 | $160,622.61 | $25,093.20 | $12,702.44 | $12,390.76 | $102,079.83 | $199,038.57 | $147,920.17 |
| 13 | $147,920.17 | $25,093.20 | $13,756.74 | $11,336.46 | $115,836.57 | $210,375.03 | $134,163.43 |
| 14 | $134,163.43 | $25,093.20 | $14,898.54 | $10,194.66 | $130,735.11 | $220,569.69 | $119,264.89 |
| 15 | $119,264.89 | $25,093.20 | $16,135.11 | $8,958.09 | $146,870.22 | $229,527.78 | $103,129.78 |
| 16 | $103,129.78 | $25,093.20 | $17,474.32 | $7,618.88 | $164,344.54 | $237,146.66 | $85,655.46 |
| 17 | $85,655.46 | $25,093.20 | $18,924.68 | $6,168.52 | $183,269.22 | $243,315.18 | $66,730.78 |
| 18 | $66,730.78 | $25,093.20 | $20,495.42 | $4,597.78 | $203,764.64 | $247,912.96 | $46,235.36 |
| 19 | $46,235.36 | $25,093.20 | $22,196.53 | $2,896.67 | $225,961.17 | $250,809.63 | $24,038.83 |
| 20 | $24,038.83 | $25,093.20 | $24,038.83 | $1,054.37 | $250,000.00 | $251,864.00 | $0.00 |

A graphic method of showing principal versus interest is included in the next chart. The upper bar of interest is nearly 80% of the initial year's payment. By the final year, the payment is nearly all principal.

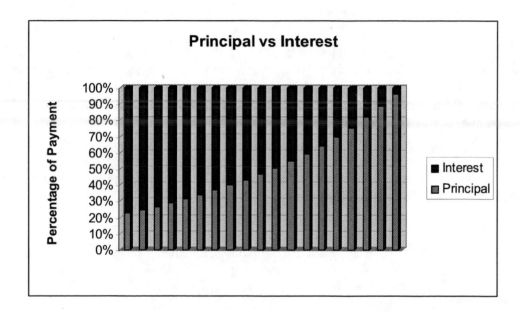

## Fully Amortized VS Partially Amortized

The amortization period and the loan repayment term are not always the same length of time. As we explained with balloon payments, a loan may be amortized for a longer period of time than the repayment, but require a balloon payment of the principal balance at some pre-determined date.

A fully amortized loan is a loan where the amortization period and the loan repayment term are identical. At the end of the amortization period, the borrower owes nothing on the loan. As shown in the previous example, both the loan term and the amortization period were 20 years. At the end of 20 years, the principal balance on the loan was zero.

A partially amortized loan, in comparison, has a longer amortization period than the repayment term of the loan. This type of loan generally requires a balloon payment because there is a principal balance at the end of the repayment term. The benefit to a partially amortized loan is that the interest rate charged by the bank is often less than the rate that would have been charged on a fully amortized loan.

**Example 1**:

Comparing a fully amortized 10 year loan for $250,000 to a partially amortized loan, amortized over 20 years but requiring a balloon payment in year 10.

| Loan Type | Amortization Period | Loan Term | Monthly Payment | Interest Paid in 10 Years | Loan Balance in 10 Years |
|---|---|---|---|---|---|
| Fully Amortized | 10 Years | 10 Years | $3,033.19 | $113,982.80 | $0.00 |
| Partially Amortized | 20 Years | 10 Years | $2,091.10 | $173,283.56 | $172,351.56 |

In this example, the borrower still owes $172,351.56 at the end of 10 years. Why would this scenario be better for a borrower? The borrower's payment is nearly $1000 less per month. The borrower may not be able to budget for the higher expense for the first few years of operation. This partially amortized loan is perfect for some clients.

**Example 2**:

Comparing a fully amortized 15 year loan for $250,000 to a partially amortized loan that is also amortized over 15 years, but requiring a balloon payment in only 5 years. The borrower is given a 1% rate reduction for these terms.

| Loan Type | Amortization Period | Loan Term | Interest Rate | Monthly Payment | Interest Paid in 5 Years | Loan Balance in 5 Years |
|---|---|---|---|---|---|---|
| Fully Amortized | 15 Years | 15 Years | 9.00% | $2,535.67 | $102,310.28 | $200,170.08 |
| Partially Amortized | 15 Years | 5 Years | 8.00% | $2,389.13 | $90,263.43 | $196,915.63 |

In this example, the borrower has the benefit of a slightly lower monthly payment and additionally pays over $12,000 less in interest over the first 5 years of ownership.

# Calculating Mortgage Payments

As you're in the field with prospective buyers or investors, many will ask you roughly how much a payment on a particular property will be. Be prepared to calculate payments using Microsoft Excel or a financial calculator.

## Using Microsoft Excel

Using Microsoft Excel, you can determine a mortgage payment with the following formula:

**= PMT(Rate, Nper, PV)**

Rate = The Interest Rate divided by 12 months.
Nper = The number of total payments (ex: 20 yr loan = 20 yr x 12 mo = 240 payments)
PV = Amount borrowed.

Example:  Calculate the Payment for a $250,000 mortgage based on an 8% loan rate for 20 years.

= PMT( 8%/12, 20x12, 250000)
Rate = 8% / 12 months; Nper = 20 years x 12 months, PV =$250,000.
$2091.10

## Using a Financial Calculator

Our example uses an HP 10b calculator.  Most HP calculators work in a similar fashion.

| Key Stokes | Display | Description |
| --- | --- | --- |
| Press **12** , **SHIFT** , then **P/YR** | 12 | Sets to 12 payments per year |
| Press **250000** , then **PV** | 250,000.00 | Stores loan amount of $250,000 |
| Press **20** , **SHIFT** , then **xP/YR** | 240 | Stores number of months for the loan |
| Press **0** , then **FV** | 0 | Stores 0 as the loan balance in 20 yrs |
| Press **8**, then **I/YR** | 8 | Stores monthly interest |
| Press **PMT** | -2091.10 | Calculates monthly payment |

# Calculating Maximum Purchase Price

Your investor has determined that he or she will not buy the property unless he or she can purchase it for $1800 per month or less.  The investor is willing to put down $50,000 on the purchase.  If the current rate is 8% on a 20 year fixed rate loan, what is the maximum purchase price the investor will pay?

## Using Microsoft Excel

Using Microsoft Excel, you can determine the maximum price with the PV formula:

### = PV(Rate, Nper, Pmt)

Rate = The Interest Rate divided by 12 months.
Nper = The number of total payments (ex: 20 yr loan = 20 yr x 12 mo = 240 payments)
Pmt = The maximum mortgage payment.

---

= PV( 8%/12, 20x12, 1800)
Rate = 8% / 12 months; Nper = 20 years x 12 months, Pmt=$1800.
$215,197.73

---

## Using a Financial Calculator

Our example again uses an HP 10b calculator.

| Key Stokes | Display | Description |
|---|---|---|
| Press **12** , **SHIFT** , then **P/YR** | 12 | Sets # payments per year |
| Press **20** , **SHIFT** , then **xP/YR** | 240 | Stores the number of months for the loan |
| Press **0** , then **FV** | 0 | Stores 0 as the loan balance after 240 months |
| Press **8** , then **I/YR** | 8 | Stores interest rate |
| Press **1800**, [ **+/-** ], then **PMT** | -1800 | Stores desired payment (money paid out is negative) |
| Press **PV** | 215,197.73 | Calculates the loan an $1800 payment buys |
| Press [ **+** ], **50000** , then [ **=** ] | 265,197.73 | Adds $50,000 down payment for total purchase price |

# Understanding the Loan Process

Although there are many types of commercial loans and a variety of lenders, most loans are processed in the same manner. There are several individuals or groups who touch a loan while it is being processed:

- **Originator or Loan Officer** - An originator or loan officer is the person who takes the loan application and initially pre-qualifies the buyer. This may be the manager at a local bank, or it may be a mortgage broker working independently in the area. The originator collects the initial documentation necessary for processing the loan, and in most cases passes the loan package on to a processor.

- **Processor** - A processor, or processing team, takes the loan package that was filled out by the originator and begins to determine what additional information may be required to approve the loan. The processor collects information on both the buyer and the property, including full credit reports, copies of leases, property appraisals, title reports and financial statements. The processor then packages the loan and submits it to the underwriter for approval. If the loan company is a mortgage company, the processor may actually "shop" the loan to several lenders in order to find the best loan terms for the borrower.

**LOAN PROCESS**

**Originator** or **Loan Officer** fills out an application

↓

**Processor** orders an appraisal to determine the value of the property, obtains copies of information on the borrower and property, and prepares a loan package for underwriters.

↓

**Underwriter** reviews the loan package and approves or rejects the loan, or requests additional information. If approved, the Underwriter then issues a commitment letter.

↓

Loan is closed and money disbursed at settlement.

- **Underwriter** – An underwriter is the decision maker in the loan process. In some lending institutions, such as community banks, the underwriter is actually a committee that decides on the loan's approval or denial. At times, an underwriter will request additional documentation or verifications in order to approve a loan.

Once the loan is approved, the borrower will receive a **commitment letter** outlining any remaining conditions of the loan. Conditions may include clear title to the property, final verifications of employment or the payoff of another loan.

# Types of Lenders

Commercial mortgage lenders come in every variety, shape and size. They range from large commercial banks and insurance companies to private individuals who invest in trust deeds. The lines between various types of lenders often blurs because mortgage brokers tend to use a variety of sources to find loans for their clients. Commercial lenders typically fall into the following categories:

- **Commercial Banks** – Most Commercial Banks are **Portfolio** lenders. They write and fund commercial mortgages and retain them as part of the bank's portfolio, rather than selling the loans on a secondary market

- **Life Insurance Companies / Pension Funds** – Also Portfolio Lenders, Life Insurance Companies and Pension Funds invest in commercial mortgages for the return generated by the mortgages. Other Portfolio Lenders include some Real Estate Investment Trusts (REIT).

- **Commercial Mortgage-backed Securities** – Commercial mortgage-backed securities, referred to as CMBS, are a type of bond commonly issued in security markets. CMBS are a type of security backed by commercial real estate. CMBS loans typically feature pre-payment penalties to the borrower that reduce the likelihood of the borrower refinancing the property. These loans are often sold and serviced by **conduit** lenders on behalf of the investors.

- **Private Lenders** – Often referred to as "Hard Money Lenders", Private Lenders and Private Lending Groups are often willing to take on a higher risk loan than institutional investors or CMBS loans. In return, these lenders or groups require a higher interest rate or higher return on the money that they loan. In some cases, private lenders are more concerned with the value of the property and their return than the actual qualifications of the borrower. Hard Money loans are often used by borrowers as a temporary method of securing the property, by accepting a high interest rate loan and attempting to refinance it at a later time.

- **Sub Prime Lenders** - A sub prime lender is one who funds loans that do not qualify for "typical" commercial bank loans or other portfolio loans. Sub prime loans tend to be higher in rate than conventional bank lending rates. Some sub prime lenders are independent, although most are affiliated with or owned by commercial banks and lending institutions. The primary difference between conventional commercial bank portfolio loans and sub prime loans is that the bank or lender is willing to loan money to a borrower with a lower-than-acceptable credit score or on a higher risk property as long as the borrower is paying a higher rate of interest and often significant up-front fees to the lender.

- **Specialty Lenders** – Some properties are difficult to finance because the underwriters have a difficult time understanding the business. Specialty Lending accounts for much of the lending for unique properties, such as Assisted Living Facilities, Resorts, Marinas, and other properties. This kind of lending may be done by commercial banks or lenders with background in each of the specialty fields, or may be private groups of investors with familiarity of how each type of property operates.

# Types of Commercial Loans

Commercial loans may be used to purchase a commercial or investment property, refinance a property, or develop a property. Most lenders have different rules for each category of commercial lending. For example, lenders are more willing to refinance a performing asset than writing a purchase loan for the asset because the lender can view a track record for the owner with this particular property.

Types of loans include:

- **Purchase or Acquisition Loan** – Used for the purpose of acquiring a property. The purchase loan is typically provided in one sum to the borrower at the time of settlement for the property acquisition.

- **Blanket Loan**- A loan that covers several properties owned by the same party.

- **Development Loan / Subdivision Loan** – A loan that funds the subdivision of a property into smaller parcels or funds the redevelopment of a parcel into a different use. A development loan may include financing for improvements to the parcel such as roads and utilities. Development loans are often released in "draws" at certain intervals set up between the lender and borrower as certain benchmarks in the development process are reached.

- **Construction Loan** – Although a construction loan may be part of an overall development loan, a construction loan may also be a simple loan to build a structure on a land parcel or add to an existing structure. Construction loans are also typically released in "draws" as benchmarks are reached. A draw might be used for the land acquisition, a second draw when the foundation is complete, a third draw when the framing is complete and so on.

- **Refinance Loans** – A refinance loan pays off an existing loan against the property with the proceeds of the new loan. This is often done by borrowers in order to secure a lower interest rate or better lending terms.

- **Cash Out Refinance Loans** – A refinance loan that lends the borrower more than the original mortgage, allowing the borrower to leave settlement with additional funds.

- **Subordinate Loan** – A loan in a "second place position" or third place. In the case where a borrower already has a mortgage on a property and requires additional funds for repairs, renovations or other purposes, a lender may make an additional loan on the property. These subordinate loans are generally at a higher rate than conventional mortgages. In the event of a default, the subordinate mortgage is less likely to receive the full value of their investment back.

# Qualifying for a Commercial Loan

Commercial lenders review the qualifications of the borrower including credit worthiness, income, and experience. However, there are two or three ratios that a lender requires a property and borrower to meet in order to fund the loan.

## Loan to Value Ratio (LTV)

The Loan to Value Ratio is simply the mortgage amount divided by the appraised value of the property. In the process of obtaining a loan, the lender orders a commercial appraisal, which is often very expensive and is done at the borrower's expense. The appraised value, or Fair Market Value, is set by the appraiser and reviewed by the loan underwriter.

Although LTV's can fluctuate depending on the borrower's experience, credit and income, commercial loans generally require 20% or greater down payments. A 20% down payment is the same at an 80% Loan to Value Ratio.

$$LTV = Loan\ Amount\ /\ Appraised\ Value$$
$$LTV = 100\% - Down\ Payment\ Percentage$$

Different risk categories of property may also require greater down payments, resulting in a lower LTV. Lenders may require purchasers of higher risk businesses, such as taverns, or higher risk industries, such as coal mining, to put more money down and prove their experience in operating that type of business.

## Debt Service Coverage Ratio (DSCR)

A Debt Service Coverage Ratio is a calculation of how much of the property's net income is used to cover the debt service, or principal and interest payment of the proposed loan. It is a calculation of cash flow of the property. The calculation is:

$$DSCR = Net\ Operating\ Income\ /\ Debt\ Service$$

For example, if a 10 unit office building were generating a Net Operating Income of $62,000 per year, and the buyer was planning to borrow $450,000 at 8% for 20 years, the yearly principal and interest payment on the loan would be $45,168 per year.

$$DSCR = \$62,000 / \$45,168$$
$$DSCR = 1.373$$

This means that the property generates $1.37 for each dollar in debt. A DSCR of 1.373 would be high enough for most lenders and situations. Like LTV, the Debt Service Coverage Ratio varies depending on the business type or industry of the property being purchased. Typical industries require a DSCR of between 1.2 and 1.35.

## Debt Ratio

The last ratio used in commercial lending is the Debt Ratio. This ratio is the personal debt to income ratio for the borrower. It is calculated by dividing the borrower's monthly debt by the borrower's monthly income. A percentage of income from the property being purchased may be added to the borrower's monthly income to help the borrower qualify.

This ratio is not commonly used in the purchase of commercial and investment properties unless the borrower is planning to use the property for their own business. Most lenders are concerned about the income and expenses of the property itself. In the case where a borrower is planning to purchase a commercial property to open a restaurant, house his telemarketing staff, or create any owner occupied business, the lender will be weigh the borrower's credit worthiness more heavily and the borrower's ability to repay the loan regardless of whether or not the business venture succeeds. This is partly done through a debt ratio.

# Commercial Loan Applications

Although every lender is different, most require standard information about the borrower and property. The following are generally required documents for commercial loans:

Personal and Business Information:

- Tax returns – most recent three years including personal and business returns.
- Bank Statements – most recent three months.
- Personal Financial Statement – updated within 60 to 90 days.
- Schedule of Real Estate holdings.
- Year to Date Profit and Loss Statement for any business ventures.
- Letters of explanation for any derogatory credit.
- Personal resume and specific information on management of any business or property that can be related to the property being purchased.
- Copies of any LLC, LLP or corporation paperwork if property is being purchased in the name of a partnership or corporation.

Property Information:
- Profit and Loss Statement for the property.
- Copy of prior owner's most recent two years tax returns.
- Rent roll and unit description of the property.
- Copies of all leases.
- Property Insurance information.
- If retail-tenant occupied investment property, include financial statements on tenants.

Business Information (if purchasing or starting a businesses):
- Resume of all management experience.
- Business Plan – full explanation of the plan.
- Business Projections.
- Copy of franchise agreement, if applicable.
- Outline of competitors.

# Summary

A full understanding of the commercial mortgage process is necessary to assist buyers in evaluating their options when considering the purchase of a property. The view point of the buyer, or borrower, is different than the lender. Borrowers consider a loan to be a debt, while lenders consider a loan to be an investment. Lenders come in all shapes and sizes, and their loan rates and fees depend on the risk inherent in the property and in the borrower.

Important aspects of the lending process include a broad understanding of how amortization works and the difference between full amortized loans and partially amortized loans that require a balloon payment before the end of the amortized period.

Lenders are concerned with the loan-to-value ratio of the property, which is based on the mortgage amount divided by the appraised value, and the debt service coverage ratio which is calculated by dividing the net income by the annual mortgage payment.

## Chapter 5:  Review Questions

1.    True or False:  The term "Balloon Payment" refers to a situation when a borrower is able to pay a large chunk down on their mortgage balance.

2.    The Legal Promise a borrower makes to the lender that they will pay back the loan is called the:

     A.    Promissory Note
     B.    The Mortgage
     C.    Deed in Trust
     D.    Mortgage Note
     E.    None of the Above

3.    Using a financial calculator, calculate the Payment for a $375,000 mortgage based on a 7% loan rate for 25 years.

4.    Your investor has determined that he or she will not buy the property unless he or she can purchase it for $2400 per month or less.  The investor is willing to put down $60,000 on the purchase.  If the current rate is 8.5% on a 20 year fixed rate loan, what is the maximum purchase price the investor will pay?

5.    The ratio of the amount borrowed against a property to the appraised value of the property being secured by a mortgage is called the:

     A.    Mortgage to Value Ratio
     B.    Loan to Value Ratio
     C.    Loan to Appraisal Ratio
     D.    Mortgage to Appraisal Ratio
     E.    Debt Ratio

6.    A buyer has a Shopping Center under contract for $7.5 million.  The buyer is borrowing $6 million for the project on a 20 year loan at a rate of 6.75%.  The Net Operating Income of the Center is currently $627,000 per year.  What is the Debt Service Coverage Ratio of the property?

7.    The loan officer who takes a mortgage application is known as the

     _____.

8.    The final approval or denial of a commercial mortgage comes from the

     _____.

9. Using Excel, create a spreadsheet of the Amortization Schedule of a $375,000 loan at 10% for 10 Years. How much total interest is paid in the 10 years?

10. A lender who funds loans that do not qualify for "typical" commercial bank loans at a higher in rate than conventional bank lending rates is known as a:

A. CMBS
B. Specialty Lender
C. Subrogated Lender
D. Sub Prime Lender

# 6

## The Practice of Commercial Real Estate

All Real Estate transactions, whether they are residential or commercial, begin with a buyer and a seller, or a landlord and a tenant.  While it's true that commercial and investment real estate involves far more mathematical calculations, projections, legal complications and financing alternatives than its residential counterpart, the industry is not nearly as complex as agents fear it to be.

On the owner's side of the transaction, you'll be working either with a property seller who wants to sell or a property landlord who wants to rent a property.  On this seller side or landlord side of the transaction, there are three basic components: prospecting, presentation and service.  All aspects of marketing and selling or leasing commercial or investment real estate falls into these three areas.   On the buyer side or tenant side of the transaction, there are also three basic components: prospecting, presentation and service.

### The Seller's Side

For the sake of simplicity, whether you're working with a property owner or business owner who is considering selling their commercial or investment real estate, or you're working with a property owner who wishes to lease part of the property, you're working with an owner.  You will prospect to find these owners, who may have need of your services, using the same methods.  Your presentations and servicing of sellers or

| The Seller's Side |
|---|
| 1.  Prospect<br>    * Find Potential Sellers |
| 2.  Presentation<br>    * Marketing Presentation<br>    * Pricing the Property<br>    * Handling Objections |
| 3.  Service<br>    * Provide Feedback<br>    * Call Regularly<br>    * Market & Advertise |

landlords will also be very similar. As a commercial real estate professional, you are trying to obtain a 'listing contract' for the lease or sale of their property or business, and you are then trying to market that listing to potential buyers or tenants. Your goal is to obtain the best sales price, lease rate or situation for your property or business owner.

In dissecting the seller side of the transaction, prospecting is the first job of any successful commercial realtor. The number one reason that any real estate professional fails is failure to prospect for business. You'll find that I repeat that mantra throughout the practice section of this text. Prospecting for sellers can involve hundreds of different target audiences or groups and dozens of methods and strategies for approach. As a new commercial real estate professional, you must make some choices. You can use a scatter-gun approach to prospecting by attacking every different property type and market. It makes far more sense, though, to select the target audience and method of approach to that target audience that most fits with your personality and situation. A target audience might be owners of office buildings, or owners of shopping centers or even farmers with land to develop. We'll discuss this in detail in the next chapter.

Presentation, the second part the owner's side of the transaction, includes several components. You'll need to make an effective presentation to the potential client, of course. But you'll also have to evaluate the marketability and potential sales or lease price of a property or business. Further, you'll need to handle objections the owner will raise during your presentation and your analysis of the property. Keep in mind that every owner thinks their property is better than every other owner.

The final piece in the seller puzzle is delivering service to your seller. Service includes maintaining ongoing communication until their property is sold or leased, creating a specific targeted marketing plan for the property and providing feedback from potential buyers and tenants to the property. The service component will also include negotiating a contract in your client's best interest.

## The Buyer's Side

Almost a mirror of the seller side, a prospective buyer or prospective tenant must be located, then shown why they should work with you, and then serviced. On the seller's side of the transaction, a commercial realtor will advertise to promote their listings and attract buyers or tenants. Your goal is to handle those incoming inquiries and convert them to buyers or tenants who will work with you to find the perfect

| **The Buyer's Side** |
|---|
| 4. Prospect<br>　* Convert Calls |
| 5. Presentation<br>　* Qualify Buyer / Tenant<br>　* Buyer Agency<br>　* Handling Objections |
| 6. Service<br>　* Find/Show Properties<br>　* Analyze Market |

location. Unfortunately, most realtors convert only a small percentage of incoming calls into clients. Using careful techniques to determine the buyer or tenant's wants and needs can go a long way to converting a larger percentage of calls into clients.

A buyer presentation includes pre-qualifying the potential client to determine if their wants and needs are in line with their ability to finance. There's little worse than wasting a few weeks of time finding the perfect location for a client, only to discover that the client can't really afford the location. A presentation to a buyer must also include discussion of buyer agency and why buyer agency is in the best interest of the client.

The last component of working with buyers or tenants is servicing their needs. The service component will include showing properties, analyzing each location and determining the value of the possible locations to the buyer or tenant.

# The Sale

Putting together a sale involves writing offers for buyers and presenting offers to sellers. As a real estate professional, you'll have to negotiate any agreement in your client's best interest. Additionally, if the agreement is contingent upon financing, zoning or inspections, your job will be to assist in coordinating all the players involved in the transaction, and possibly renegotiating the deal depending on the outcome of the inspections or zoning approvals.

7

# Prospecting

## Introduction to Prospecting

It was February 11th and I was in my mid-20's without a date for Valentine's Day. I had recently broken up with a long-time girlfriend and wasn't sure what to do next. So I went to the local florist and ordered a dozen roses. I then asked the florist to send one rose to each of twelve different young women I had selected. The florist said "*You're kidding, right?*" I wasn't. That's called prospecting. Select a target audience and let them know you have something to offer them.

My experience with training several hundred Realtors over the years has taught me that prospecting is the hardest part of any real estate career. The number one reason that Realtors fail in this industry is that they fail to schedule the time to find prospects. This is particularly important early in a Realtor's career. In the long run, Realtor's who deliver exceptional service receive many referrals from their clients, which limits the amount of prospecting successful Realtor's need to do. However, when building a real estate business for yourself, you need to look at the various options available to seek out qualified property sellers and buyers.

Again, the number one reason people fail in real estate is that they don't begin a prospecting program when they first begin their career in real estate. Your goal is to create a steady flow of business into your pipeline. That can be tougher than it sounds, especially when you're getting started in your new career.

Certainly most new agents, as they venture into this endeavor, expect that the company will generate leads for them. While it is true that most good real estate organizations generate some buyers, sellers, landlords and tenants simply from the advertising done by the company, you will not make a great living at any company waiting for the phone to ring. That is the kiss of death in the commercial real estate industry.

Over the long term, what you want to do is build a steady flow of referrals from your past clients, business associates, friends, and even relatives that will keep you going forever. It's a process to create those referrals, and you have to survive long enough in the industry, making a living, until you have a database of people who like and trust you that will continually feed and expand your business and client base.

In the beginning of your career, however, you need to proactively find sources of leads for sellers, buyers, investors, landlords and tenants. There are three forms of finding business in real estate:

- **Reactive** - Waiting in the office on floor time or opportunity time for the phone to ring so you can pick up a client. You will never become rich waiting for the phone to ring. You will be at the mercy of the market.

- **Pro Active Long Term Marketing** – Long Term Marketing is generally another passive form of seeking clients. Mailings, postcards, and similar methods generally produce very few immediate clients. Regularly mailing to organizations or individuals who are likely to buy, sell or expand in the future may bring business to an agent in the future. Joining referral or community organizations and promoting yourself regularly may bring future business as well.

- **Pro Active Short Term Prospecting and Marketing** – An agent who is actively seeking companies or individuals who need their assistance right now is pro-actively short term prospecting.

One of the great aspects of working in the Real Estate industry is that you can create your own business within a business, without the overhead of running a small business. This is an industry where you'll need inventory in order to survive. Your inventory is your portfolio of properties for sale or for lease. However, unlike most small businesses, you don't have to pay the carrying costs for purchasing inventory to sell. You're marketing someone else's product and being paid for that service.

Unless you are independently wealthy, in the beginning of your career, you're going to need to find clients who need to buy or sell right now. That might mean sitting down and calling every property owner along Main Street in your city or every business in an industrial park to find out if they're considering expanding, moving or selling. It might mean stopping by every business in several office buildings to meet the owners and ask if they need assistance in their growth plans. Knowing that you probably have to go out and make cold calls or knock on doors is a hard pill to swallow for most new agents. However, you won't have to do it forever. You are building a business for the long haul. As you treat these clients with professionalism, honesty and give them 100%, they will refer you business and your personal business will grow.

"But Loren," my new agents usually start, "can't I just start mailing brochures and postcards and stuff to the owners of businesses? Won't that work?"

Our experience is that if you mail huge volumes of material out to prospective clients, you will get some prospects. Our return has been about 1/10th of 1%. So if you mail to 1000 prospective clients, one might contact you, and a contact doesn't mean they're going to use your service. As with any marketing or advertising, if you mail consistently over and over again to the same group, they will eventually begin to recognize your name and services. That may take a year to eighteen months to start generating any possible business. Most new agents can't survive a year and a half without income.

What I recommend to new agents as they begin their journey into the world of commercial real estate is that they select two target markets and two prospecting methods their first month in the business, and grow from those two methods. One of the methods should be long term, and one should be short term. The best long term method, I believe, is to start consistently contacting your sphere of influence. Those are the people who already like and trust you. For short term prospecting, there are many methods that we'll discuss over the next several pages.

# Long Term Prospecting Methods

Long term prospecting involves the creation of a client base or a database of clients, consistently staying in touch with that client base, and offering them your services.

## Sphere of Influence

You probably know at least 100 people that you see from time to time. You have family, friends, old acquaintances, former co-workers, college roommates and even the doctor, dentist and hair dresser that you see on a regular basis. You may not realize it, but these people are the beginning of your client base. As

---

### Sphere of Influence Prospecting

**Step 1** – Compile a list of 100 acquaintances.

**Step 2**- Get their addresses, phone numbers and email (if possible) and enter them into a database.

**Step 3** – Write an initial letter explaining you're in Real Estate and need their help finding clients.

**Step 4** – Follow up in 2 weeks with a "Properties for Sale" flyer.

**Step 5** – Follow up in 2 more weeks with a "Recent Sales" flyer.

**Step 6** – Send everyone a personal handwritten note in the first 90 days.

**Step 7** – Schedule ongoing mailings.

your career grows, you'll add past clients, business associates and new contacts to this client base.

Agents scoff at the idea that their 68 year old Uncle Albert could possibly assist them in the listing or sale of multimillion dollar office buildings. The truth is that every person you know has their own internal database of people they connect with regularly. Almost 20 years ago, I met a man who was living in a roach infested tenement. This man referred me to a client who owned several hundred properties in Pennsylvania. You will never know who you can connect with until you start asking for help from those around you.

Also, you already know people who own commercial property or operate small businesses. You'll never know precisely when your Uncle Otto is going to sell his Scandinavian Restaurant. And wouldn't you be crushed if Otto listed their business with Ex-Lax Realtors, the one's who have diarrhea of the mouth, because he didn't remember you were in real estate? Don't let that happen - stay in front of your sphere of influence!

And please avoid saying, "I don't need to send anything to my family and friends. They all *know* what I do." Because they really have no idea what you do. The truth is that as much as your Aunt Petunia likes you, at this point in your career, she's probably not going to refer you to her old high school boyfriend who is now President of the local bank. Why? Unfortunately, Aunt Petunia, like all your relatives and friends, remembers you from your prior career. She can't visualize you as a successful commercial realtor and she doesn't want to potentially damage her present relationships by telling them about an unproven new realtor.

It's not that Aunt Petunia and Uncle Albert don't love you. They do. But they are afraid that if you, as a new commercial realtor, make a mistake, it will come back to haunt them. One of our most successful techniques at my firm has been to assist agents in appearing successful before they actually *are* successful. This technique involves keeping you in front of your sphere of influence, but also showing your sphere of influence some evidence of production.

To start, you'll need to create a database of all those people you have some contact with. Collect all the names, addresses, phone numbers and email addresses for everyone that knows you. Enter that information into a database program. There are several commercially available programs such as Microsoft Outlook and ACT that you can pick up at your local Office Depot or Staples. There are also programs specifically designed for the real estate industry, such as Top Producer. The key is to get a database put together quickly so that you can begin contacting the database consistently.

First, you need to announce that you have entered the exciting world of real estate, and second, you'll need to convince your sphere that you are the "go-to" person for anyone needing assistance. We recommend that during your first 90 days in the business, you contact your sphere 6 times, or about once every two weeks. After your initial 90 days, you should follow up with your sphere at least once a month, if not more.

Your initial letter should be simple and to the point. Example:

---

Dear Aunt Petunia,

      As you may know, I've made a career change. I'm now a licensed Commercial Real Estate Agent and I've affiliated with one of the top firms in Eastern Pennsylvania, Century 21 Keim Commercial and Investment Realtors.

      In order to obtain my license, I had to complete several courses and pass a State Exam. I took this education over the past few months. To join Century 21 Keim, I've had to take a lot of additional education, but I think it's all been worth it. Real Estate is an exciting business!

      I'm hoping you'll help support me in my new endeavor. If you hear of anyone thinking of buying or selling property, please call me. I'll include a few of my business cards with this letter. Please put them in your wallet or purse and give them out to anyone you can.

      Remember, although I may be new to the industry, I've had a lot of education and training, and I'm backed by some of the top people in Commercial and Investment Real Estate here at Century 21 Keim.

      Thanks!

---

Your second letter should show some evidence that you are actually working to sell properties. Honestly, by your second or third week in the industry, it's unlikely you'll have any listings, so you'll need to "borrow" some. You're going to send out a flyer that displays two or three different properties for sale, with your name and company name on the bottom of the flyer. You don't actually say anywhere that the properties on the flyer are your listings, but your sphere of influence will assume they are, and their impression of you will hopefully shift. The reaction you're looking for is "*Wow, John seems to be doing well after only a few weeks*".

Ask around your office to find out if anyone would mind if you send copies of other agent's listings with your name on them to your clients. It's rare that an agent will tell you that they don't want you exposing their property to a few hundred people in your database.

# Do you know a buyer for any of these properties?

**Center Square Easton Office Building** – Over 11,000 square feet of Class A office space only one block from the waterfront, this exceptional property features a bank on the first floor, and four large office suites on the second floor. A great investment offering a wonderful return. **Offered at $1.59 Million.**

**Senior retirement home / Assisted Living Facility** plus retirement village. Village has 44 home sites. 31 pad sites are rented at $302 per month (per owner). Assisted living facility contains 44 bedrooms and can potentially house 88 residents. Facility includes full Kitchen, Dining Hall, offices, elevators, 44 bedrooms, salon and a Living Room on every floor. **Offered at $3 Million**.

**Service Station with Gas** – 3 Bay Service Station with new gas tanks, and successful long term business. Sale includes real estate, business, and equipment including three lifts and a computer diagnostic system. **Asking $599,900**

**A photo of you will go a long way to associating you with the properties!**

**For More Information, Please call:**
**Your Name**
**Your Firm**
**Cell: 000-000-0000**
**Office: 000-000-0000**

At this point, you should begin sending personal notes to everyone you know. Purchase a few boxes of blank note cards from your local office supply store. Then set up a time each morning to write 5-10 personal handwritten notes. If you send out 5 each day, you'll hit 100 people in your database in just 20 work days. Your goal is to let them know you're thinking of them, and personally ask them for assistance.

One of the other amazing things I've discovered of top agents across the country is that almost all the top agents I've met follow a regiment of sitting down every morning between 7:30 and 9:00 and writing out between 5 and 20 personal handwritten notes. Personal notes really connect and resonate with people. If you plan to continue the practice after your initial wave of notes to your sphere of influence, and you should, you may have to really think hard each day of who you want to write to and what you can say, but it will keep you in the forefront of many people's minds.

**Sample personal notes:**

| | |
|---|---|
| Hi!<br><br>I'm waiting for a client at the office today and have a few extra minutes. I thought I'd jot you a quick note.<br><br>Thanks so much for speaking with me the other day. It's truly refreshing to work with considerate people. | Hi!<br><br>I was thinking about you today, so I thought I'd write you a quick note. I just wanted to say thanks for all the little things you do for others… |
| Hi!<br><br>Thanks for considering using my services, it really means a lot to me… | Hi!<br><br>I was just going through my files today, and realized how long it's been since I spoke with you! I love working with fun people like you… |

About two weeks after sending the initial flyer with 3 properties for sale, try sending a similar one that displays 3 sold properties. The headline of this flyer could read "Successful Sales by Our Team!" and the tag line on the bottom of the flyer could say "If you know of anyone thinking of selling a commercial or investment property, please have them contact me." Again, even though you are honestly telling people that your firm sold properties; your sphere of influence will naturally read this to say that you just sold 3 commercial properties.

This will lead to your family and friends talking about how well you're doing in such a short period of time. Again, your entire goal is to convince them that you are the person to refer, and this will typically do it. Build on your initial letters with similar marketing pieces over the first year. Keep in constant contact with this group, and add to the group continually as you meet new people.

## Client Gatherings

In this industry, like many others, you need to create a steady flow of referrals in order to keep your business going. In order to create that steady flow of referrals, you need to survive long enough in the industry. Remember that Real Estate is a relationship game. The stronger your relationships, the more referrals you will generate and the stronger bonds you'll make. Don't fall into the trap of selling a property and neglecting the client after the sale. Your clients can be your strongest advocates for your personal business.

Your ongoing mail program will go a long way toward building those relationships, but there's nothing quite like the personal touch of getting together with your clients periodically. As I've talked to super producers around the country over the years, one of the common elements I've found is that super producers typically have regular client events. Some have yearly summer picnics for their clients. Others have holiday parties, or even a movie night periodically where they buy 200 tickets at a discount. The important part of the equation is regularly finding a way to be physically in front of your clients.

One of our top agents started doing a summer picnic at her home for her friends and clients the first year she was in business. She has expressed that it's one of the greatest things she does for her business. Not only does she have fun and enjoy the company of her clients away from business, but her phone rings with referrals after every client gathering. She has now started doing a winter wine and cheese get together as well so that she touches the group twice a year.

## Farming for Business

The most commonly discussed long term method of prospecting is farming. A farm can be a geographic area, such as a particular office park or a part of town, or it can be a business type, such as gas stations, assisted living facilities, or hotels. The downside to farming is that you will need to contact the same group of businesses or individuals over and over until they begin to recognize you. It may take a year to eighteen months to actually see any results from your work. The upside to farming is that once you become known as the specialist in that area or property type, it becomes very difficult for another realtor to unseat you.

For example, one of my primary specialties was commercial horse farms. I had chosen that type of property as one that I thought was being ignored by the established real estate brokers. I began mailing continually to that group, showing up at equestrian events, developed websites, and published a newsletter about commercial horse farms. Over time, I took over that market because I was the *specialist* who really understood the market.

After several years of selling these commercial horse farms, I was referred by one of my clients to list a very large Assisted Living Facility. Rather than refer the listing to another associate, I researched the Assisted Living marketplace and found that the most likely buyer would be one of the investor groups that owned other Assisted Living Facilities. I sent out flyers about the facility that I had listed to everyone who owned such a property in the tri-state area, and received enough inquiries that I sold the property very quickly. I then followed up with a "sold" flyer to the same group, stating that I still had buyers looking for similar facilities and to contact me if they were considering selling. I received 3 more listing calls on similar properties.

My team has done the same thing with restaurants, gas stations and other properties where an owner wants to deal with an "expert" that really understands their particular situation.


## Workshops

Another great source of business can be created by marketing yourself as the local expert in some niche market. One of the best ways to set yourself apart as the expert is to hold workshops on subjects that would interest your target audience. While hosting a workshop, you are immediately seen as the expert in the field.

For example, if you're already mailing to everyone who owns a restaurant with a liquor license, you can create a mailing announcing an upcoming workshop on issues related to selling or financing restaurants or liquor licenses. "How to sell a restaurant without holding any second mortgage" might be a possible topic. You may even find a commercial mortgage broker who would be willing to split the cost of the event with you.

If you're concentrating specifically on selling commercial investments, such as multi-user office buildings or retail strip centers, you may want to target doctor's groups, attorneys and other possible investors. Contact the local hospitals to set up a workshop in the hospital for the employees on "How to Invest in Commercial Real Estate", "How to Leverage your Assets to Increase Your Investment Portfolio" or "How to Find Great Tenants for your Commercial Property."

## Networking Organizations

When you first enter the field of commercial real estate, you have time. Use that time wisely, and get yourself in front of as many decision makers as possible. Join any local community groups that make sense. Go to the local Chamber of Commerce Meetings and local planning meetings.

Another good source of leads for our associates has been to join networking or business builder groups, like LeTip. LeTip is a national organization with local chapters. Each chapter only allows one person in from each business category. For example, there can only be one chiropractor, one heating and air conditioning vendor and one payroll specialist. The group tries to grow each others businesses, and presses each member to "tip" the other members with possible leads. These types of groups can help multiply your efforts to get your name out in front of potential clients. Additionally, each person in a LeTip group is probably a decision maker in a business, and these may be potential buyers and sellers for you in time.

## Other Networking

There are many other professions that are closely tied to commercial real estate. My team receives regular referrals from local attorneys because they often speak with clients about their needs before the client contacts a realtor. Commercial mortgage brokers, bank lending departments, architects, geologists, engineers, surveyors and zoning officers are all great sources of leads.

# Short Term Prospecting Methods

All of the methods in Long Term Prospecting are effective at building lasting relationships with clients that can help your career to blossom, as long as you continue to deliver good service to your customers. However, in order to stay in the business long enough for the long term methods to work for you, you'll need to generate an income by creating some short term business. You need to make it a priority to find buyers and sellers who want to buy or sell right now. If you don't, in six or seven months your spouse will be telling you that you'd better go out and get, yes you guessed it, "a real job".

Short term systems include prospecting expired listings, properties and businesses for sale by the owners, and just plain cold calling or door knocking to find the people or businesses that need to move now.

## Cold Calling

I realize the absolute most avoided activity in the real estate industry is cold calling. However, if you don't have a large book of business currently, including lots of listings and a regular stream of buyers, investors and prospective tenants knocking down your door, you need to start building a career somewhere.

Select a few target markets and create a reason to call. For example, your firm may have recently leased a vacant office space in an industrial park. Ask the listing associate if they mind if you prospect that industrial park for other units to lease. Then make a list of all the buildings around the firm's recent contract, and locate the owner's phone numbers.

No, I didn't say locate the owner's mailing address. Remember that most mail will be thrown out without being opened. In order to survive in this industry, you need to find business now. Pick up the phone and start calling the owners or decision makers of the surrounding properties.

"Hi, this is Simon Bonapart calling from At Your Service Commercial Realty. I'm just calling because we recently leased a space in a neighboring building to yours. We found a few prospective tenants while marketing that space, and I'm just calling to see if you know of anyone else in the park that might be considering leasing or selling some of their space."

If the person you're speaking with asks you how much the space leased for, they may be considering leasing some of their own space. Make sure to follow up with a Personal Note Card and thank them for being so pleasant on the phone.

You might also try the simple and direct approach. "Hi, Mr. Smith? This is William Shakespeare calling from Your Friendly Neighborhood Commercial Realty. I'm trying to find properties for my firm to market. I was just wondering if you were considering selling your building or if you needed assistance finding any tenants?"

One of the top agents in our firm started cold calling right out of the starting gate. His first day in our Allentown office, he sat down and told me that he had four kids to feed.

He selected all the multi family properties in one particular zip code and simply called them. "Hi, Mr. Carrigan? My name is Bobbie Papageorgiou. I'm a real estate investor in the area. I'm actually also an investment specialist at Century 21 Keim Commercial Real Estate. I'm sorry to bother you, but I noticed you owned some property near mine. I was wondering if you were considering adding to your portfolio by buying more properties, or if you were considering liquidating – selling off properties while the market is fairly hot?"

This was a strong approach because many investors are either planning to add more properties to their portfolios or start selling off what they own. Using this script, Bobbie was able to find both property buyers and property sellers with one set of phone calls. The cold calling technique helped him to jump-start his career.

## Vacant Property Owners

There are investors who buy vacant land parcels in commercial and industrial areas because they want to develop them, but their plans change before the construction. You will also discover investors who buy the land for speculation; simply to hold onto until some future date. In either case, these are very good prospective listings.

Search your local tax records for vacant land that is zoned for commercial, industrial, office or even multifamily uses. Call the owners and ask them if they're planning to build on the land or if they're planning to sell the land. "Hi, Mrs. Johnson? This is June Cleaver calling from Hometown Commercial Real Estate. I came across your property on Alberdeen Drive today while I was researching other properties. I was curious if you planned to build on that site or if you were planning to sell it?"

A few years ago, I was asked to attend a meeting in Virginia. On a whim, I looked up all the vacant land parcels in the part of Pennsylvania that I was servicing that were owned by companies or individuals in Virginia. I sent out a note to all of them announcing that I'd "*be in their area*" for a meeting and if they were considering selling their property in Pennsylvania, I'd love to meet. I then followed up with phone calls. Ultimately, I scheduled seven listing appointments all over the eastern part of Virginia, and left for Virginia two days early. I listed four of the properties in just over a day because the clients were pleased that I could meet them in person.

## Expired Listings

Expired Listings are properties that have been on the market with competitors for a period of time without selling. These properties have been taken off the market by the owners, or their listing contract with their realtor has expired. Expired listings can often be found in the local Multiple Listing Systems, or by carefully tracking online databases like LoopNet to determine when a property vanishes from the system.

Many of these properties are listed again with another real estate broker within days of the property being taken off the market. Most expired listings come back on the market within a year, unless seller's plans have changed or they're unrealistic about the price. Once a company or group decides to relocate, retire or expand, they generally *do* move. Even if they take a few months off in between realtors, they typically re-list the property at some point.

Calling or stopping by the owner's of expired listings can be a quick method of capturing listings. As with any other form of prospecting, make sure if you're going to target expired listings, that you do it consistently. Don't simply take a hit or miss approach by calling the expired list one time, or once in a while and expect it to work. Consistency is the key to any long term success.

## Other Methods

There are literally dozens of methods to finding immediate business. Every time you drive by a construction site, you're driving by a potential listing for sale or for lease. You can look in the newspaper for any businesses advertising "by owner" that they're retiring, you have a possible target. Each time you read an article stating that a company has expansion plans, you have someone to contact.

These are all people or companies raising their hands saying "Hey, I'm here and I'm planning to expand, sell or lease." You may get a lot of rejection in the beginning. You may have to knock on a lot of doors. But you will find business. It's everywhere. It's actually hard not to trip over it as you drive through your town or city. You need to start making contacts and building your book of business.

I once read about a Real Estate firm that had 25 agents and 25 telephones, but no desks. When agents worked in the office, they would have to stand. The broker claimed it was a very effective strategy because he wanted the agents out on the streets actually knocking on office doors and doing something. I'm not sure how long I'd be able to maintain a staff if they had no place to sit down, but the story indicates the importance of getting out there and meeting people because that's where your business really is. This is a people business. This is a relationship business. This is relationship game and you have to meet people.

## Summary

As you begin your journey into the adventure that is the real estate industry, you must set time aside to prospect for clients. Some of that prospecting should be "long term" using methods such as farming areas or farming types of properties, joining networking organizations and consistently mailing to your sphere of influence. Long term prospecting is effective because it builds a residual effect by creating an image in consumer's minds that you are the person to call for commercial real estate.

Long term methods often take 12 to 18 months to start generating results. In order to survive long enough in the real estate business for your long term prospecting to work, you need to focus on some short term methods as well. Short term methods include calling the "expired" listings of other agencies, owner's trying to sell on their own, and even cold calling.

Prospecting will be a key ingredient to your success. Without it, you will likely become one of the statistics of the industry.

# Chapter 7: Review Questions

1. True or False: The number one reason that real estate agents fail is a failure to prospect.

2. All of the following are Short Term Prospecting methods except:

   A. Cold Calling
   B. Calling Expired Listings
   C. Calling For Sale by Owners
   D. Farming
   E. All of the Above are Short Term methods

3. True or False: Farming for business usually results in listings and sales within 3-6 months of starting the farm.

4. True or False: Your Sphere of Influence mailings should be limited to those people you know who already own a business or commercial property.

# 8

## The Listing Presentation

### Introduction to Listing Commercial Properties

There are several steps to consummating a successful listing of a property. The first step is getting an appointment, which requires prospecting as outlined in the last chapter. The second step is to research the property and the local marketplace so you are prepared to meet with the owners. You must then put on a great presentation outlining your marketing and servicing program, and handle any objections that might be voiced by the owners. You must also work to price the property so that it is competitive with other similar properties. Last, you must understand all the paperwork associated with listing a property including a listing contract, any local consumer notices or seller's property disclosures and a closing cost estimate.

The key to selling any piece of commercial real estate is to list it correctly. If you can get the property owner to allow you to openly market the property to all potential buyers, to price the property correctly for the current market and location, and to make repairs to show the property in its best light, you are far more likely to sell the property during the term of the listing. Rather than taking a listing for the sake of taking a listing and arguing with the owner later about lowering the price, allowing signage or cleaning up the property and making repairs, you need to be honest with your clients at the initial interview.

Being honest with a property owner about the value of his or her property is often difficult in competitive markets. Too many of your competitors will give the owner an outrageously high suggestion of list prices because they want a sign in front of the property. A sign will lead to buyers, who may be switched to other properties and create income for the agent. This is not in the best interest of your property owner. You are forming a sort of partnership with your client to get the property sold. As with any partnership, I feel it's always better to be honest from the outset. If you lose a listing to a competitor because the client has been seriously misled by your competitor, you may get the listing back later with better terms as the first listing expires.

## The Listing Track

The presentation is not what you do in front of the client the day you make your marketing and servicing "pitch", but rather everything you do up to and including that formal presentation. My suggestion is to send or drop off a pre-listing package prior to your initial meeting with the owner. At the meeting, you should qualify the property owner to determine whether the owner is serious about using your services to sell or lease their space, then all the facts and data about the property, as suggested in Chapter 2. Next, go through your formal marketing and servicing plan with the owner, and hopefully handle any objections at that point. You should always discuss price last, because you want the client to select you based on your skill, your marketing and your service, not because you told the owner a price they wanted to hear. An important component of a complete presentation is the approach to the client, how you carry yourself, and what questions you ask the seller.

Our goal is help you to have a greater ratio of success on your listing appointments by teaching you the principals behind the appointment. Every few weeks an agent will come up to me and say something like "I lost a listing because another agent put the listing on some web site, or *XYZ Commercial Realtors* produces their own magazine."

The truth is a whole lot deeper than any particular advertising program. And please let me explain up front that I've built a career on specific targeted advertising, but advertising is not what the owner of the property wants. There are four fundamental truths that most real estate agents ignore and never learn.

| **The Listing Track** |
| --- |
| 1. Send out a Pre-Listing Package |
| 2. Gather Data |
| 3. Show up promptly for your appointment |
| 4. Smile |
| 5. Qualify the Owner's Motivation, Needs and Desires |
| 6. Review the Property |
| 7. Marketing Presentation |
| 8. Handle Questions |
| 9. Review Pricing |
| 10. Sign the Listing Contracts and required disclosures |

First, the property owner really doesn't care about advertising. They care about getting their property sold or leased. Selling is what they want, not advertising. The second truth is that far too many property owners or decision makers see Realtors as *salespeople* lying in order to talk them into doing something they don't want to do. They often have difficulty viewing you as a professional. Over time, this image will change as more and more of your business is referred to you, but right now, the customer doesn't know you.

In order to obtain the listing on each appointment, and to list it correctly, you always have to think from the spot of the property owner. You want to be their trusted advisor, or a family friend, and you can't do that until the client both likes and trusts you. If they don't like and trust you, they *will not* see you as anything other than a salesperson.

Here's the third truth. This property is probably one of the owner's most valuable assets. They have a lot of emotion tied up in the property. They really believe its worth more than it really is, and you are the enemy who is going to tell them they can't get what they want. Worse, they're interviewing 3 other agents, and one of them is from Full of It Realtors where they fib to clients continually. That agent is going to swear to them that they can get even higher than they want, and most sellers will list with the person who gives them the highest price, because emotionally, people buy into the higher price.

The fourth truth is that in the back of their mind, they think the building will probably sell itself and they've considered trying to directly sell it. Because they think the property will sell itself, they think that you are not worth that 5%, 6% or 7% they *think* you receive.

We want you to do what's right for the client, and what's in the best interest of the client. And what's in the best interest of the client is telling that property owner the truth. They need to know the truth about marketing, the truth about service and the truth about pricing it correctly. We also want to build a long term relationship with this client so that they are so excited about our service that they refer us their family, friends and co-workers forever.

In order to accomplish this, you cannot look like every other agent that walks into their lobby. Clients may be sold on your company before you get past the receptionist. They may be sold on your marketing or you may have leased the neighbor's building for them. But once you're in the door, the owner will list with whoever they connect with the most, or whoever gives them the highest price. A typical owner is interviewing between 3 and 4 agents. You need to create a better edge, and show them that you are not the typical agent who is *just* interested in sticking a sign in front of their office building or shopping center. You have to *show* them that you want to be their trusted advisor, and that's a challenging thing to accomplish.

The track outlined over the next few pages is a sequence of events that assist you to build a bridge to show the client that you really care, and that you are the best person for the job of leasing or selling their property.

153

# Pre-Listing Package or Resume Book

Effectively, a Pre-Listing Package is a resume book. By resume book, I mean actually physically putting together a binder with lots of stuff about you and your firm in it. Remember that in order to be viewed as a trusted advisor, you need the client to both like and trust you. It's nearly impossible to get someone to like and trust you in one meeting just by speaking with them. You have to show yourself to them.

One way to do this is to create a book about yourself and your career. Actually, as you get busier in this industry, you'll find that you should probably have 4 or 5 copies of a book about yourself and your career. This is one of those things you're just going to have to trust me about. Have some blind faith.

Here's the sad and scary truth. Property owners will make a snap decision about you when they first meet you. For whatever reason, they may form a poor first impression of you, and it's tough to recover from that. They may not like the way you dress. They may not like the way your hair is done. You may remind them of their uncle Mike who mooches off them regularly. Whatever the case is, if you are one of 3 or 4 agents interviewing for the position of marketing their five million dollar high tech facility, the owners are probably going to have an affinity for one of the agents they meet.

Let me give you another example. I first became licensed at 18 years old. At 21 or 22, I still looked like I was about 15, and I had more knowledge and experience than many of the agents I competed against, but I still lost on listing appointments regularly because a business owner would open the door, and decide I wasn't experienced enough. Some competitor of mine who may have been 50 years old, but with only 3 months in the business, often looked more experienced than I did. I had to come up with a way of overcoming that initial impression by the owners that I was too young.

You need to improve your odds, and change business owner's and property owner's attitudes toward you before you even meet. One way of accomplishing this task is to find common ground with the sellers. A resume book can be a 3 ring binder full of stuff about you. And by stuff, I mean a lot of color and a lot of photos. You can take *stuff* and put it into plastic sleeves, and fill up a binder.

## Introductory Letter and Company Profile

Start your book with an introductory letter about yourself and how you put your customers first. The next few pages should always be a profile of your company, highlighting the company's accomplishments, experience of the owners or partners, years in business, size of staff, and range of company marketing. Then outline a basic company marketing plan and include lists of websites you use, databases you belong to, and memberships your firm is part of.

Next, put in some photos of yourself. You can ask someone to take a photo of you in front of your office. Put the photo in your book with a little description or caption below. Have a photo taken of you in front of a huge commercial real estate sign. Include a photo of you holding some coveted real estate award? Okay, so it's not your award, but the photo shows you as a successful professional.

## Agent Credentials

You are interviewing for the position of marketing a property. As with any interview, you should include a resume. An outline of your education, copy of your license, copy of your board membership and any awards may be included in this section.

## Testimonials

Next put in letters from people saying you're the best. You may be too new in the business to have testimonials. However, there are many mortgage brokers and bankers who want you to use them and would like nothing more than to write how wonderful you are. All you have to do is ask them for help. Once you're in the business six or seven months, the brokers from your competition will call and tell you how wonderful you are in order to recruit you. Ask them to put it in writing and add it to your book.

---

**Sample Testimonial Letter:**

Dear Candice,

Being a commercial mortgage professional in the industry, I meet many commercial and investment real estate agents and brokers.

I just wanted to write you a quick note to let you know what a privilege it is to work with someone as professional and knowledgeable as you are, Candice. You are diligent, responsive, and yet very patient with your clients. You clearly take pride in doing a great job. And of course, you are both professional and personable.

There are many rough spots on the road to closing a commercial real estate transaction, and I believe any client would be lucky to have you to help navigate the road.

Thanks again,

Bill Freeman
XYZ Commercial Funding

---

## Properties for Sale

You may put in photos of commercial properties that your company has sold in the area to show evidence of your success. Make sure these pages are in color in order to highlight your marketing. You may want to have several pages available to alternate depending on the type of appointment. If you're attempting to lease an office building, you may want to include properties that were leased in the area by you and your firm. If you're trying to list a medical facility for sale, you may want to try to select any medical facilities ever sold by the firm to prove your success in that arena.

## Personalizing your resume

And most important, include some photos of you doing the activities you love. That's the most important thing that can be added to the book, because you want to show the property owner that you are a person not a sales person.

If you golf, put in photos of you golfing. Golfers love to talk to golfers. If you bowl, add bowling photos. If you have a dog or a cat, put a photo in the book. Cat people love cat people. Put in photos of your kids. Humanize yourself so they can see you as that person. I realize this probably sounds corny to you, dear reader, but have a little faith. This may be the most powerful technique you use in your career.

Make sure to drop off the book or have it delivered a day or two ahead of the listing appointment. Why do that? Because you want to give them time to see you in the book.

One of our top agents for years had been Ellie Barrett. Ellie had an amazing gift of connecting with people. When I went to listing appointments with her, she would walk into the lobby, and find some connection with the property owner before we sat down in a conference room. Photos of kids on the owner's desk would lead her to talk about her daughter, and maybe her daughter had been in the same activities as the owner's kids. She always found a connection. "Oh, you used to supply parts to AT&T? I used to work at AT&T."

Most of us don't have that same gift. So we have to find another way to build a connection with the business owner or property owner. When you drop off a resume book, the *client* will find the connection *for* you and ask you about it when you get to the actual appointment. Now here's my warning.

# Working in Teams

Another way to improve your first impression with the client is to work in pairs. A few years into my career, I started working with a young lady named Mae Diamond. Mae worked as a good foil with me because some owners prefer men and some owners prefer women. We could often play off each others strengths and cover each others weaknesses.

You may want to consider working with a partner, particularly in the beginning, until you become a strong listing agent.

When I worked with Mae, I would cold call properties in areas where we had recently sold one to find owners who were interested in a market evaluation. Once I would get an appointment, Mae would actually call the owner back before we got there. She called for two reasons. First, she was helping to build rapport with the clients in order to help them like and trust us. Secondly, she was collecting data and gathering information on the property so that we'd have a basis to run some comparable sales.

The most interesting aspect of Mae, though, was that she had a killer way of breaking the ice with a client. The most difficult part of any meeting with a property owner is the impact of that initial meeting with the client and their initial impression of you. When an owner would open the door, or meet us in a lobby, Mae would say something about how after talking to them she felt like she'd known them forever, and she'd give them a hug. Yes, I'm not kidding, she would actually hug them. That would break the ice instantly, and we virtually never lost a listing.

Now, I'm not suggesting you go out and start hugging all your clients, because most of us would be beaten senseless. But I will suggest that you find your own way of breaking the ice with clients, and that you use a resume book or pre-listing package as part of your technique.

# The Presentation

On the day of your presentation, it's critical that you arrive at your appointment *on time*. Don't be early and don't be late. Be on time.

Paste a smile on your face before you enter the lobby, or ring the door bell, or get out of your car. Why? Too many commercial brokers attempt to create a business-like look for themselves, and they look like they're frowning. Honestly, you don't look professional, you look constipated. Put on a big smile.

Follow the property owner to their office, conference room, or any place where you can sit down. I always attempt to sit down with the client prior to viewing the property. This is important for two reasons. First, you want to break the ice with the client, if possible. More importantly, in order for the client to believe that you want to do what's in their best interest, rather than just "get the listing", you have to show them that you care about their wants and needs. Sit down and ask them questions about their situation. Don't try to sell them on your marketing, experience or techniques at this point. Just ask questions and listen.

It's also very important to take notes and actually write down what the owner tells you. This is important so that you can remember everything later, but it's also important to show the client that you care enough to take notes about their situation.

Once you have a clear understanding of the client's situation, ask if you can view the entire property. As they walk you through the property, make sure to notice and write down the positive features of the property. Try to ask questions about the property and the owner's history with the property.

When you arrive back at the owner's office or conference room, after the tour, pull out your marketing and servicing plan. Briefly explain that you don't want to waste the owner's time, but you do want to explain how you and your company market property like theirs and how you service your customers by keeping them informed of every step in the process.

The property owner may tell you that he or she knows you have a great marketing program, but he or she is really just interested in your opinion of the price. You need to explain that too often a client selects an agent based on the price told to them by the agent. In order for a commercial property owner to make a good decision on selecting a real estate firm to market and sell or lease their property, they really need to make their decision based on the strength of the firm's marketing and servicing plan. They should never make a decision based on hearing a particular price.

As you're putting together your marketing and servicing plan, you should either put it together as a book that you can step through with the client, or as a Powerpoint presentation. People are visually oriented. They remember far more of what they see than what they hear.

Although presentations will vary from company to company and area to area, some of the inclusions I suggest as either slides or pages in a book include:

1. Marketing your property on the Internet
2. Marketing your property through MLS systems and Commercial Databases
3. Staging your property to attract the highest offer prices
4. The Pitfalls of Commercial Financing for your property
5. Protecting your interests through Due Diligence Periods

As you're putting together your PowerPoint presentation, or your presentation manual or book, always keep in mind that as you present this to the property owner or the company decision maker, you are being compared with other agents and firms. We've tried to set ourselves apart from the competition by dropping off a resume book or pre-listing package ahead of the appointment and showing the client that we care about their situation and understand their situation by asking questions, listening and taking notes. But the actual presentation should build on this strong foundation. Make sure your presentation explains what differentiates you from your competition.

1. What unique services do you or your firm offer?
2. What unique marketing programs or systems do you have access to?
3. In what way is your company different from other commercial real estate firms?

4. How can you communicate these differences to the clients in a way that resonates with the clients?

Much of my team's success has been due to our ability to display the tools that many agents use, and position those tools as exclusive guarantees. For example, we've offered our clients our guarantee that if they are unhappy with our service, we will allow them out of a listing after a certain period of time. This lowers the barrier of resistance to signing a long listing contract. Many of our competitors offer the same thing, but few actually give a "Service Guarantee" form at a listing presentation.

There are many possible tools that you can turn into exclusive guarantees. Consider what your company offers their clients, and re-think how to position those offers in the mind of the customer. Consider how to differentiate your services from those of your competition. You may surprise yourself and your customers.

One last note about the presentation: as mentioned earlier in this Chapter, many property owners or business decision makers don't believe they need us to market their properties. In fact, many owners believe that we simply add the property to a database and sit back, waiting for it to lease or sell. If we can show them the "problems" that occur in a transaction, namely commercial financing issues, renegotiations that happen during due diligence periods, and similar issues, they are more likely to see the value in hiring us to assist them through the process.

# Pricing the Property Correctly

The next key element in selling a property for top dollar is to price the property correctly in the beginning of the listing. Unfortunately, virtually all property sellers I've dealt with have wanted more than the property would sell for. It takes a lot of skill and effort to help owners to understand that their properties may not be worth quite as much as they'd like.

My favorite line from a property seller is "I'm not going to *give* my building away!" I've heard that line probably 200 times. I often wonder if all commercial real estate owners watch the same reality TV show, because they all come up with the same lines.

Please don't misunderstand me. I do not want a seller to under price their property and give away some of their equity. However, I also don't want to overprice the property and scare away good potential buyers, or price the property so high that it's not competitive with other properties in the marketplace. Remind owners that you are paid on commission. The higher sales price or lease rate you negotiate on behalf of the owner, the more money you make.

Another consideration is that if a property sits on the market too long, it becomes stale. If it becomes stale, the owner may actually end up selling the property for less than they would have if it were priced right from the beginning.

Owners often feel that they can price a property on the high side, and a buyer who likes the property will make an offer. "And after all, I have the best corner in the entire metropolitan area…" It amazes me how many commercial property owners appear to believe that. The truth is that most buyers or investors look at a dozen or more properties before making a decision. These buyers or investors may get a good feeling about your seller's property, but they'll make an offer on the one they feel is the best value, so if your seller's property is priced above some of the competition, you may not get any offers at all.

What I tell property owners is that I honestly don't price properties. I don't. The open market prices them. All I can do is to give a property owner an educated guess as to what buyers are likely to pay. The individuals that truly determine a property's value are the buyers. They set the value or the price by looking at similar properties for sale or lease during the same period of time your property is for sale or lease, and offering on those properties.

As I compare prices of other properties with the owner, I extract a Market Analysis form from my materials. I explain that there are three different types of comparable properties. The first are those properties that are currently for sale. Those are the seller's competition, and we should not price a property above similar competing properties in the marketplace unless there is some extraordinary factor. The problem with using just properties currently available is that some of those properties will never sell or never be leased, because some of them are overpriced.

The second group are those properties that have recently sold, or been leased. These properties show us what buyers and investors in the market are actually willing to pay for a property of similar qualities. The last group is expired listings, or properties that didn't sell, or were not rented during the term of the listing, and that generally tells us what "too high" is when pricing a property.

## Investment Property Market Analysis

| Address | List Price | Sales Price | Days on Mkt | # Units | Price / Unit | NOI | Cap Rate |
|---|---|---|---|---|---|---|---|
| **Properties for Sale** | | | | | | | |
| 123 Apple Valley | $365,900 | | 11 | 8 | 45,738 | $32,700.00 | 11.19 |
| 457 W. Church St | $375,000 | | 9 | 8 | 46,875 | $32,450.00 | 11.56 |
| 1504 Fernwood | $439,900 | | 37 | 10 | 43,990 | $45,000.00 | 9.78 |
| 241 N. Loop Road | $329,900 | | 121 | 7 | 47,129 | $28,710.00 | 11.49 |
| 19 Upstream Rd | $450,000 | | 88 | 9 | 50,000 | $41,200.00 | 10.92 |
| 99 N. 23rd Street | $299,900 | | 17 | 6 | 49,983 | $27,475.00 | 10.92 |
| **Properties Recently Sold** | | | | | | | |
| 15 Berger Way | $459,900 | $452,000 | 96 | 10 | 45,200 | $44,200.00 | 10.23 |
| 127 Alberdeen Rd | $375,000 | $372,000 | 28 | 8 | 46,500 | $36,500.00 | 10.19 |
| 19 Scotts Drive | $499,900 | $470,000 | 115 | 10 | 47,000 | $45,000.00 | 10.44 |
| 78 2nd Avenue | $325,000 | $310,000 | 34 | 7 | 44,286 | $29,100.00 | 10.65 |
| 783 Andover Road | $429,000 | $415,000 | 19 | 8 | 51,875 | $38,800.00 | 10.7 |
| 11 Bittner Way | $275,000 | $270,000 | 27 | 6 | 45,000 | $28,200.00 | 9.57 |
| **Expired Properties** | | | | | | | |
| 995 Pear Road | $500,000 | | 180 | 10 | 50,000 | $45,200.00 | 11.06 |
| Old Carriage Way | $399,900 | | 120 | 8 | 49,988 | $34,275.00 | 11.67 |
| 525 Vine Street | $474,900 | | 172 | 8 | 59,363 | $42,100.00 | 11.28 |
| 55 Farmingdale | $335,000 | | 150 | 6 | 55,833 | $28,900.00 | 11.59 |
| 987 Debbie Lane | $450,000 | | 164 | 8 | 56,250 | $40,100.00 | 11.22 |
| 910 Chestnut St | $310,000 | | 180 | 6 | 51,667 | $26,500.00 | 11.70 |

# Types of Listing Contracts

I would love to say that all listing contracts are exclusive and you get paid regardless of who sells the property. Unfortunately, that's not true. Some clients will not allow their properties to be openly marketed, but will allow a "Showing Agreement". Other owners of commercial properties will sign Open Listing Contracts non-exclusively with several brokers, hoping one will find them the best buyer.

## Exclusive Right to Sell, Exclusive Right to Lease

An Exclusive Right to Sell listing is a contract that requires the owner to pay you, the listing Realtor, a commission if the property is sold or leased during the term of the listing contract, regardless of who was the procuring cause of the buyer or tenant. In other words, whether you ultimately bring the buyer, another Realtor brings the buyer, or the owner themselves bring the buyer, you are still paid a commission for your services in marketing the property and representing the owner.

This is the preferred listing contract for nearly every situation, because it helps you to protect your commission and locks you in as the agent representing the seller or landlord in the transaction. Any other agents or buyers must come through you in order to purchase or lease the property. If a buyer is represented by a competing agent or firm, you simply split the fee from your property owner, but you still represent the property owner's interests.

In some situations and some marketplaces, Exclusive Right to Sell listing contracts are difficult or impossible to obtain from property sellers. In very hot markets, property owners or business decision makers may be called on a regular basis by agents asking them to sell their property. Many of these sellers will tell agents to bring them an offer and they'll consider it. Realtors run into similar situations with particular property types as well. Beachfront hotels, for example, are called on a regular basis by buyers and agents asking about the possibility of selling.

## Exclusive Agency

An Exclusive Agency listing contract differs from an Exclusive Right to Sell in that the owner may sell the property without paying a fee to the agent. If the buyer who purchases the property, or the tenant who leases the property, is introduced to the property by any real estate broker or firm, the listing broker is paid a commission. If the owner finds their own buyer, the agent is not paid.

### Open Listing

In some marketplaces, agents take Open Listings, where a property owner may list a property with several or many real estate agents or firms. Whichever real estate firm brings the buyer or tenant for the property collects the entire listing and selling commission. If the property owner finds their own buyer or tenant, no agency is paid.

## Showing Agreement

When property owners are hesitant to sign any sort of listing contract, but are willing to consider offers, you may have to resort to having the owner sign a blanket showing agreement that states the owner will pay you a commission if you bring an acceptable agreement of sale. A one-time showing agreement states that the owner will pay you a commission if one particular buyer or tenant, who is introduced to the property by you, purchases or leases the property in a certain time period.

---

**SAMPLE:**

### Broker's Fee Agreement / Showing Agreement

**Owner / Seller of Property**: _____

Broker: _____

Licensee(s) _____

**PRICE:**

Asking Price of Property (if applicable) : _____

**PROPERTY DESCRIPTION:**

Address _____

Municipality (city, borough, township) _____

County _____

Zoning _____ Present Use _____

Property Identification -Tax ID#; Parcel #; Lot, Block; Deed Book, Page, Recording Date)

_____

**The following Client(s)** have been identified by **Broker** as potential buyer(s) of **Owner's Property**:

_____

**BROKER'S FEE**

Broker's fee is _____% of the sales price AND a fee of $_____, paid by Seller. Broker and Seller have negotiated the fee that Seller will pay Broker

**PAYMENT OF BROKER'S FEE**

Seller will pay Broker's Fee if the Property, or any ownership interest in it, is sold or exchanged to any Client, identified above, within _____ days of the signing of this Fee Agreement.

**NOTICE TO OWNER**

If Owner / Seller has any questions or concerns about this Contract, Owner is instructed to seek legal advice from an attorney.

---

# Parts of a Listing Contract

A written listing contract is a legal contract between you, as the Realtor, and the owner. In most areas, standard listing contract forms for commercial real estate are available from either the local association of realtors or the state association of realtors. Some large real estate firms have developed their own versions of commercial listing contracts.

Because a listing contract *is* a contract, there are certain elements that must be included to create something that is both legal and binding on both parties[13].

1.  **Name of all Parties** – The owner or owners of the property and the real estate broker or firm.

---

Owner / Seller of Property: _____

Broker / Company representing Property: _____

Licensee(s) _____

---

2.  **Asking Price for Sale or Lease** – Although some agents do list properties with price ranges, or "bring all offers", a contract should have a specific list price. The owner is offering the sale of or use of a property in return for compensation. That compensation should be spelled out.

3.  **Description of Property** – Address, tax parcel information and a description of the property in order to avoid any confusion.

---

**PROPERTY DESCRIPTION:**

Address _____

Municipality (city, borough, township) _____

County _____ School District _____

Zoning _____ Present Use _____

Property Identification -Tax ID#; Parcel #; Lot, Block; Deed Book, Page, Recording Date)

_____

---

[3] All clauses and contracts included in this section are used expressly for the purpose of providing examples to the reader. Any actual legal contracts or clauses require the consultation of an attorney.

4. **Contract Length** – This clause should outline start date of the contract and the end date or expiration of the contract.

---

**STARTING & ENDING DATES OF LISTING CONTRACT (ALSO CALLED "TERM")**

A. Starting Date: This Contract starts when signed by Broker and Seller, unless otherwise stated here:

_____

B. Ending Date: This Contract ends on _____

---

5. **Broker's Fee** – The fee for securing a successful sale or lease of the property should be clearly spelled out on the listing contract. If the fee is a range based on price or based on whether the sale or lease is consummated by the listing agent or an outside agent; that should be spelled out as well.

---

**BROKER'S FEE**

Broker's fee is _____ % of the sales price AND a fee of $_____, paid by Seller. Broker and Seller have negotiated the fee that Seller will pay Broker.

### COOPERATION WITH OTHER BROKERS

  Licensee has explained Broker's company policies about cooperating with other brokers. Broker and Seller agree that Broker will pay from Broker's Fee a fee to another broker who procures the buyer and who:

  A: **Represents Seller as a Subagent**  Broker will pay _____ of / from the sale price.
  B. **Represents the buyer as a Buyer's Agent.** Broker will pay _____ of / from the sale price.
  C. **Does not represent either Seller or Buyer.** Broker will pay _____ of / from the sale price.

---

6.     **Payment of Broker's Fee** – Always include a clear explanation of the fee in order to protect your commission.

---

**PAYMENT OF BROKER'S FEE**

Seller will pay Broker's Fee if the Property, or any ownership interest in it, is sold or exchanged during the term of the Listing Contract by Broker, Broker's salesperson, Seller or by any other person or broker, at the listed price or any price acceptable to the Seller.

Seller will pay Broker's Fee if a buyer is found by Broker or by anyone, including Seller, who will pay the listed price or more for the Property, or a buyer who has submitted an offer accepted by Seller.

Seller will pay Broker's Fee for a sale that occurs after the Ending Date of this Contract IF:
(1) The sale occurs within _____ days of the Ending Date, AND
(2) The buyer was shown or negotiated to buy the Property during the term of this contract.

If a sale occurs, Broker's Fee will be paid upon delivery of the deed or other evidence of transfer of title or interest. If the Property is transferred by an installment contract, Broker's Fee will be paid upon the execution of the installment contract.

---

7.     **Legal Notices** – If your state requires a consumer notice to be provided to the property owner, either that notice should be included in the listing contract, or an allusion to that notice. Additionally, because most commercial real estate professionals are not attorneys, a notice should be included to instruct the seller to seek legal counsel if they have any concerns.

---

**NOTICES TO OWNER**

Broker and Owner have complied with all state required Consumer Notice and Seller's Disclosure laws. Broker and Owner have executed all documentation required by the state.

If Owner / Seller has any questions or concerns about this Contract, Owner is instructed to seek legal advice from an attorney.

---

# Handling Objections

The longer you are in the real estate industry, the more objections you will hear from prospective clients. There are several, however, that you will hear repeatedly. The objections most often spoken are about commission being too high or the suggested list price being too low. We'll discuss a few different responses to common objections below.

When you hear any objection, however, try not to take an immediate defensive stance. Our goal is to educate our prospect or client to help them make good decisions. Listen carefully to the objection. Repeat the objection, and then use a story of someone who thought the same way as your client to illustrate your point. Use facts and figures when necessary, but try to illustrate an example of a similar situation that may help the client to view the situation from another perspective.

## Real Estate Commission Objection

"The commission rate is too high." Before we discuss how to handle commission objections, legally I need to inform you that all commissions are negotiable between the broker and owner. Although certain commission rates may be "common" in any particular marketplace, they are still always negotiable and must be viewed as such. Having explained the legality, there are many great methods to handle commission objections. This is one that has worked most successfully for our associates.

Client: "Bad Breath Commercial Realty was just here, and they told me I'd only have to pay a fee of 4½% for listing my property. Why is your fee so much higher? Would you be willing to list it for less?"

Agent: "So you're most concerned about our fee?"

Client: "It's one of the things I'm most concerned about. If my building sells for $750,000, the difference of 1½% is over $11,000."

Agent: "I certainly understand your desire to obtain the lowest commission rate. There are a few very good reasons, however, to pay a full commission. Let me give you an example. We had a listing on Industrial Drive a few months ago where we had accepted a listing commission of 4½%. Because of the lower fee, we were paying any buyer's agent that showed the property a fee of 2¼%. That's below the normal commission rate in the area, so agents were actually avoiding showing the property. The owner had a great building, but other agents simply didn't include it with the listings they would send to their buyers. Eventually, we convinced the owner to raise the commission to a full 6%, and showings finally started taking place."

Client: "I'm not hiring other agents to sell my property. I'm hiring you."

Agent: "And hopefully I'll be the one to sell the property, but the reality of the market is that I may be able to work with ten to fifteen qualified buyers at a time, and there's no guarantee that any of them will want your building. Part of our goal in marketing your property is to sell it not just to the general public, but to other real estate professionals. There are about 300 commercial agents in this metropolitan area, all with their own ten to fifteen buyers. We want to attract all of them to the property. Ultimately, the owner of this property found that he needed to sell more quickly. We raised the commission above the normal commission rate to 7%, and paid out 4% to the buyer's agents. Other agents made sure to show our listing first, and the property sold very quickly after that."

Client: "So you're saying that you won't reduce the commission?"

Agent: "Actually, what I'm saying is that I can reduce the commission a bit, but I'd be doing you a disservice. Having less showings will lead to less buyers and ultimately less money in your pocket if we can't create demand for the property. And one other thing, Mr. Smith: whatever additional commission you may pay in the end, I'll make up for it by my negotiating skill. I'm one of the best negotiators in the business locally, and I'm sure I can make you back more than that 1½% difference."

## Price Objection

Client: "I've spoken with two other agents, and one was from the oldest firm in town, Smelly Socks Commercial Agency. Both agents gave me prices that were significantly higher than the one you're quoting. Why is that?"

Agent: "You're most concerned with getting the highest price possible?"

Client: "Of course. Isn't everybody?"

Agent: "I certainly understand that. I'd want the highest price for one of my properties as well. When I first arrived here today, I explained that my goal is to help you to make good decisions. You may toss me out the door for my honesty, but I will always be honest with you. Unfortunately, the truth about the real estate industry is that agents understand that property owners, while they may be smart business people, still have emotional ties to their properties. Owners tend to list with the agents who give them the highest list price."

Client: "Well, isn't it true that I can always come down in my price, but can never go back up?"

Agent: "That's not exactly the problem. The best buyers always seem to be the first ones who look at your property right after you put it on the market. If the property sits on the market too long, it becomes stale, and agents stop showing it. If you price the property right in the very beginning, you're more likely to get two or more buyers bidding for the property and possibly sell over list price. Buyers tend to look at ten or more properties before making a decision. If they view your property and get a good feeling for it, but see other properties that they feel are a better value, being business people, they will typically bid on the one that they feel is the better value, even if they like your building and location better."

Client: "How often does that happen?"

Agent: "All the time. Actually, I had a client last year named Ted. Ted owned a pretty large office building like yours. Initially, I competed against two firms for the listing. He chose another firm because he liked the price they had given him. After six months, he cancelled his listing, because nothing was happening. I then listed the property at the price I originally quoted Ted, and we sold the property within 6 weeks for full price. Honestly, I probably could have gotten him that same price last year if he had just listed with me first. Again, I'm not the kind of agent who needs to lie to you in order to put a sign in front of your building to generate buyers for myself. My business is built on a foundation of referrals from satisfied customers, and I want to do such a great job for you that you'll refer me your friends and family when they need assistance with commercial real estate. The only way I know how to do that is by being honest from the start."

## Listing Exclusions

Client: "We want to exclude a few people from this listing contract. I don't want to be paying a commission on people that I told about the property."

Agent: "Are there many people you want to exclude from the listing?"

Client: "I'll have to look over my notes, but there are a few."

Agent: "I certainly understand you wanting to save money. Have any of these people made you an offer yet?"

Client: "No, but a couple said they had interest."

Agent: "That's fine. You are hiring me, however, because of my marketing skill. My goal is to put a great presentation together on your building that will convince buyers that yours is the property to purchase. My work may even convince some of those you contacted that this is the right property for them. Why don't we exclude them for one week. You can call all of them and let them know the property is going on the market with an agency. If they don't purchase within a week, let me have a shot at trying to convince them that your property is the one to buy."

## Summary

A great listing presentation is a critical part of your success as a commercial real estate professional. Although no agent secures every listing, there are key components to a listing presentation that will help you to be successful more often. One of the most important factors in the owner's decision making process is whether or not the owner likes and trusts you. If they don't like and trust you, they are unlikely to list with you. One method of altering an owner or decision maker's opinion of you is to first drop off a resume book or pre-listing package to the owner prior to the presentation meeting. At the presentation, you should first ask questions to better understand the owner or decision maker's goals and objectives. Have a prepared, professional presentation to go through with the client, and finish by being ready to handle the client's objections.

# Chapter 8: Review Questions

1. Write out the 10 steps to a Successful Listing Presentation:

   1 _____
   2 _____
   3 _____
   4 _____
   5 _____
   6 _____
   7 _____
   8 _____
   9 _____
   10 _____

2. All of the following should be included in your Resume Book except:

   A. Company Profile
   B. Introduction Letter
   C. Photos of you doing activities like golf or bowling
   D. Testimonials
   E. All of the Above should be included

3. The type of listing contract that requires a Realtor to be paid regardless of whether another Realtor or the seller themselves finds the buyer:

   A. Exclusive Listing
   B. Exclusive Right to Sell
   C. Open Listing
   D. Exclusive Agency

4. The type of listing contract that allows whichever Realtor lists the property to keep the entire commission is known as:

   A. Exclusive Listing
   B. Exclusive Right to Sell
   C. Open Listing
   D. Exclusive Agency

# 9

## Providing Service and Marketing to your Sellers

### Introduction to Service

While the activity that realtors actively avoid may be prospecting, the activity that realtors regularly neglect unintentionally is the delivering of service to their clients. Far too often an agent will list a property for sale or for lease, and never speak to the client again. I'm not exaggerating. I've listed several hundred expired listings over the years that were initially for sale with one of my competitors. The complaint I heard most often from these property sellers was that they hadn't heard from their agent in months, and in many cases, hadn't heard from their agent since the day they signed the listing contract.

Not all properties you list will sell during the term of the listing. Not all properties you list for lease will be rented during the term of the listing. However, if you provide your property owner with regular updates on what's happening with the property and what's happening in the marketplace, you will be far more likely to get the listing extended. Even if the owner chooses to pull the listing from you and give it to another firm, they'll be more likely to respect you if you take care of them.

Another comment I've heard from dozens of property sellers is "I don't believe the property was advertised by my old realtor… even once." The truth is that the property probably <u>was</u> advertised, but the client never saw a copy of an advertisement, so they simply assume the worst. Even worse, if the property isn't being shown, the owner assumes that the reason it's not being shown is your poor advertising because they haven't seen an advertisement.

Let your clients know what you do every step of the way. Show them what goes on behind the curtain. Your goal is to make the invisible part of the transaction visible. One method of doing this is to tell a client what you're going to do; then tell them what you're doing and then tell them what you did.

For example, when you're running an advertisement on the property, you can contact the client and let them know that an ad will be coming out shortly. You can then send a copy of the ad to the client when it comes out. A week later, you can call and discuss what reaction you received from the ad. "Mr. President? Hi, it's Hal calling again from the Commercial Real Estate Depot. We had only five calls on that advertisement we ran in the New York Times and unfortunately no one liked the location of the property. Sorry, I thought that ad would work better than it did. We're going to try something a little different next week."

Start your career the right way by setting time aside every single week to make contact with all your current clients. You should be giving your clients feedback on showings, copies of advertisements and you should keep them up to date on current market conditions. Even if there's little or nothing to report to your clients, it's important to keep that personal contact. You can talk to the client about each web site the property has been listed on, which MLS systems you're currently using, how many calls you've had and so on. Again, you're making the invisible visible to the client, showing them that you're doing something to market their property.

## Feedback on showings

Feedback is one of the cornerstones of communication. If you're showing the property yourself, try to get the buyer's complete perspective of the property. If another agent is showing the property, follow up with them and try to get their opinion of the pros and the cons of the property. Sellers want to know why a buyer didn't purchase their property. Landlords want to know what tenants are renting if they're not renting the landlord's space.

When my team is asking for feedback, we automatically ask four questions so that we can get a complete picture of the buyer or tenant's thoughts.

1.      What did you (or your buyer) like about the property, and what attracted you to look at it? (This is a question that helps us to understand how we should be marketing the property and what features we should be highlighting in our marketing.)

2.      What didn't you (or your buyer) like about the property? What would you change in order to sell (or lease) it?

3.      Do you (or does your buyer) have any interest in pursuing the property?

4.      What do you think the eventual selling price (or lease price) will be on the property? (I announce that the one who comes closest will receive a dinner for two. That way, the prospect tells us what they really think; not what they want us to hear.)

## The Golden Rule

And finally during the marketing phase, always be honest with your clients. The golden rule is to do unto others as you would want done unto you. Clients pay us for our honest opinions of what needs to be done to market and sell or lease their property. As I mentioned in the last chapter, clients will often initially select the agent who gives them some pie in the sky list price, but they truly do want our honesty.

Don't forget the client once you have their property under contract. Continue to call the client often, possibly more than once a week. Sellers and landlords often continue to be under stress until closing. Anything could go wrong, and they know it. The fact that you're calling them to keep them in the loop, and asking them if there's any way you can assist them will be very encouraging to them. This may be the time when they will refer you the most business because they truly see your service.

If the sale is contingent upon a mortgage, keep in contact with the mortgage company and make sure you're the one who calls the seller to let them know when they are cleared to close on the property. I've even gone so far as to have balloons delivered when the buyer receives their mortgage commitment from the bank. I've done that because it provides the seller with relief. I generally also send the balloons to their work place so that people around the seller will talk, asking the seller what the balloons were for. At that point, my seller's often talk about me.

After the sale, send them a sincere thank you note. Treat them like people, not commission checks. And add your now closed seller to your database of people to contact on a regular basis.

## Staging and Showing the Property

Staging a commercial property is just as important as staging a residential property. Buyers buy emotionally with their eyes and you never get a second chance to make a good first impression. I learned a long time ago that a gallon of paint costs $20, but when applied correctly, it can be worth $2000 in the sale of a commercial building. We are always in competition with other properties for sale or lease. When a prospective buyer or tenant looks at our space, we want them to sit down and write up a contract for a high number. That can be accomplished more easily if they believe this is the best space they can take.

In order to make a space appear larger, staging consultants will typically paint the offices off white, because very light colors conduct the most light and make the rooms appear cleaner, brighter, friendlier and most importantly: larger. Consultants recommend that we turn on all the lights during showings to make the space appear bright and inviting. If there is any hint of mildew or water in the air, it should be eliminated immediately.

Property owners are rarely willing to do anything on a building they want to sell or lease. However, most buyers and tenants will pay more for space, and buy or lease it more quickly, if it shows very well. One technique I've used successfully is to remind property owners that if they sold a car, they'd certainly wash it, wax it and vacuum it out in order to sell it for more money. Some of them may even tune up the car. Selling a office building or a business is very much like selling a car. Buyers buy emotionally. If something is clean and neat and tidy, they will believe that you took better care of the space.

For example, if you're leasing a vacant office space, leave a few desks behind when possible. Vacant space appears smaller to the eye than space that has office furniture. Make sure the carpets are cleaned and the small holes in the walls are filled. Tenants want to be proud of the space they'll be occupying, and in the same general location, tenants will often take a space that looks cleaner and better kept.

## Signs

Commercial properties are often located in highly visible areas. Signs are a critical part of any marketing program. We find that approximately 18% of our incoming calls on specific properties come as a direct result of real estate signs. Commercial realtors often place the largest sign allowed by zoning on their listings, because signs can lead to more prospective buyers and tenants to work with.

176

If the property being sold is an operating business, the owner may refuse to allow a sign on the property. While it is true that a "for sale" sign may adversely impact the sales from their business, it is also true that the public finds out about a business being for sale pretty quickly once advertising is done. Whenever possible, have a large sign placed on the property.

# Using MLS Systems

Whether or not to use a Multiple Listing System to market your commercial properties always starts an argument when I'm in a room with a dozen or more commercial brokers. Many commercial real estate brokers and agents believe that it is a mistake to open properties to the general MLS membership. I believe the MLS systems are invaluable tools in assisting commercial realtors in obtaining the highest price for their clients in the shortest amount of time.

There are several reasons why many commercial brokers believe the MLS hurts them rather than helps them:

First, a commercial broker can often sell certain types of commercial properties themselves without any assistance, if they take the time to make a lot of phone calls. When an agent fails to let others know about their listing, they are practicing a technique often called "pocket listing". For example, if I were to list a Holiday Inn in the Philadelphia marketplace, I would first call through every other hotel owner in the tri-state area. Several of them will usually make decent offers within a few days, netting me a quick sale. If I need to resort to advertising, I can run a generic ad about motels and receive dozens of calls from prospective buyers. This technique allows me to "double-dip" by handling both the listing side and the buyer's side of the transaction. But is "pocket listing" a property in the best interest of my client, the seller? Or am I more likely to get a higher price for my client by opening up the property to the many buyers represented by many agents, and have them bid against each other?

The second major reason many commercial brokers choose to avoid multiple listing systems is that they believe most realtors associated with the MLS are residential realtors and therefore unqualified to handle a potential buyer or tenant for a commercial broker's listings. At a recent meeting, one of my competitors actually said to me "If a deal is going to be screwed up, it will be screwed up by allowing a residential realtor into the deal". While it may be true that many residential agents do not understand the nuances of commercial real estate, and you, as the listing agent, may have to handle more paperwork or guide the buyer's agent through the transaction, you still open your seller's property up to more potential buyers.

One fact that many commercial agents seem to ignore is that the public doesn't always separate commercial and residential realtors. Many prospective tenants and buyers of commercial property visit a residential real estate office first, because it's where they believe they need to go for assistance. And the plain truth is that realtors who belong to an MLS are most likely to show their prospects and clients those properties that are multiple listed before ever trying to search out properties by any other means.

My belief is that we place huge for sale signs in front of commercial properties in order to let the world know that the property is for sale or lease, we should also be placing advertising for those same properties anywhere buyers or tenants are likely to look for property, and that includes the multiple listing systems.

# Internet Resources

Over the past few years, our top source of leads has become the Internet. The World Wide Web is often the first place a prospect will go to find commercial property. You'll need to make sure your properties are easily found.

There are several methods users employ to find property on the Internet. Many users go directly to major commercial databases, such as www.loopnet.com or www.cityfeet.com. Other prospective clients may go directly to one of the Internet Yellow Pages and try to find a local commercial broker to call. Still others use search engines, such as Google and Yahoo to find websites dedicated to local commercial properties for sale.

In order to truly attract buyers from the Internet, I suggest you employ a multi-pronged attack strategy.

## Personal Web Site

If you don't yet have a personal web site, you need to create one. Far too many consumers want to read about you before they meet you. For a few hundred dollars, you can create a beautiful several page website that outlines your background, experience, personal commitment, marketing program and even your personal listings.

## Search Engines

You'll need a personal web site before attempting to market yourself on search engines, because you need the search engines to point back to where your online pages are located. Although search engine ranking seems to change regularly, the most visited search engines currently are Google, Yahoo, Ask, AOL Search and MSN's Search. The vast majority of users on the web will either go directly to one of these search portals or use another search engine that is backed by one of these.

There are literally hundreds of different search engines available to list your site, and getting listed on the top few can be difficult. Many of them, like Google, allow a user to pay a fee to show up in a banner ad, or pay a fee per click on their ad to show up higher in rank. You will find several companies that will assist you in getting listed on the search engines and improve your ranking on search engines with techniques like hidden words, meta-tags and link exchanges. Leave this job to the experts. Your job is to sell real estate.

## Online Yellow Pages

I firmly believe that in ten years we won't have physical printed yellow page directories. I believe online yellow pages will replace them. However, physical yellow page directories are still valuable tools in today's marketplace. Unfortunately, I'm not certain yet who the online yellow page winners will be. Superpages.com appears to have a strong lead in this market, and Switchboard.com is heavily used as well, but that may change.

I would recommend making certain that you are listed in the first few online yellow pages that appear when doing a search in Google or Yahoo.

## Commercial Databases

Several competitors are vying for the position of top online resource for commercial real estate. As outlined in the section on MLS, I believe it to be critically important to list your seller's properties for sale and lease in as many venues as possible, while still being cost effective. The more places a prospect can "run across" your property, the more likely the property is to be leased or sold.

Some of the major online sources for marketing property include:

- **Loopnet** – Currently a leader in online commercial real estate, Loopnet.com allows a user to search properties for sale or lease throughout the world in virtually all commercial real estate categories including the typical categories of retail, office and industrial as well as categories like business brokerage, land sales and multifamily housing. Anyone can use Loopnet to search for properties for sale, making the system a great benefit in getting your properties in front of consumers. Paid subscribers can search recent sales for comparison and upgrade the marketing of their properties on the site.

- **CoStar** – Another leading online commercial real estate database, CoStar is targeted specifically at commercial real estate professionals. The public does not have access to the database without paying a subscription fee. However, Costar.com does provide it's subscribers with presentation tools, powerful analytic tools and a comprehensive database. CoStar allows commercial real estate brokers and agents to include their listings in the CoStar database without charge.

- **Cityfeet** – Like Loopnet, Cityfeet.com allows the public to search its extensive database of properties for sale or lease. Subscribers can upgrade the marketing of their properties to include photos and more information. Cityfeet also maintains relationships with many national newspapers and other organizations, like the New York Times and LA Times, providing the backbone of their online commercial listings, and providing your listings with an even broader coverage.

- **CIMLS** – The Commercial Investment MLS is an open system that allows you, as a commercial realtor, to enter listings without charge onto the network. The service also allows the public to search the database for free if they register.

# Brochures

A colorful well written brochure is an important component of marketing for several reasons. First, it is an easy and inexpensive way to show your property owner that you are working to get the property sold or leased. Second, you should have written information available to give out to any prospect viewing the property, and third, you should have an enticing brochure available to send out to anyone calling to inquire about the property that you are unable to convert into a showing.

A strong headline should be placed on every brochure to secure the reader's attention. This is particularly important if the brochure is being mailed to prospective buyers or tenants. Determine who your likely target audience for the property might be. If it's a medical facility, you'll likely be targeting those in the medical community. If the property is a self storage facility, you'll likely be targeting investors or owners of other self storage facilities looking for lateral expansion.

Brochures should also include photos of the property, a plat map or plot plan of the site, a location map and detailed information on the property. Remember that this document is a sales pitch about the property, continuing to sell the property in your absence, so the best features should be highlighted. Information that should always be included about possible uses of the property, zoning information, utility information, building size, lot size and anything else that may be helpful to interest a buyer in the property. Other suggestions for inclusions:

- **Investment or Multifamily Properties**- Always including information on the number of units, gross and net incomes, potential returns and cap rate information. Future projections are often included.

- **Retail or Shopping Center Properties**- Demographic information on the surrounding area including wage ranges, age ranges and population trends can be very important for retail buyers. Additionally, brochures will include ranges of rental rates, gross and net incomes, potential returns and cap rate information.

- **Industrial Properties** – Aerial photos, site location photos and access points to major highways, railroads and transportation hubs are important for industrial property. Zoning uses are also a major component of an industrial brochure.

- **Hospitality Properties** – Should always include historical information about rentals, income and expenses and future projections along with an explanation of how the current owner arrived at the projections.

- **Land Parcels**- Zoning information and potential uses are critical. Aerial photos, demographic trends and site location photos are also important to include in a brochure.

Some real estate brokers create two forms of brochure. An initial brochure may include enough information to entice the prospect into calling for an advertised additional package of information. This is a method Realtors use to get prospects to raise their hands and acknowledge they have interest in the property. A secondary form of the brochure on an investment property or retail property would be much more comprehensive and may include complete breakdowns of income and expenses, details on leases, and a pro-forma projecting potential future returns.

An important note you should add to any brochure should also be that "all information was deemed to be from reliable sources, but is not guaranteed". Although this statement will not eliminate any legal liability you may have for misrepresentation of the property, it may help show that you are acknowledging that your information and data may need to be verified.

# Faxing, Mailing and E-Mailing to Other Brokers

In most marketplaces, the buyer or tenant for your listing is far more likely to be brought to the property by another realtor from your own firm or a competing firm than directly by you. That means it is very important to keep good relationships with other commercial and investment agents in your market.

One method employed by agents to market the listing is to expose it to every other commercial agent in the market. You can create an "agent version" of the brochure on the property, which is a simplified version of the comprehensive brochure you've created. You can fax this brochure to other offices, mail a physical copy or even e-mail it. The benefit to this marketing method is that once you have a system set up to fax or e-mail a brochure to other agents and offices, it's a relatively easy to create and send out brochures on a regular basis. The other benefit is that it's one more tool in your tool belt that you can show your property owner that you're working to get their property sold or leased.

The problem is that this scattergun approach seldom generates any real prospects. Your faxed or e-mailed brochure is often ignored by most of the other agents in your marketplace. After all, we all get far too much e-mail to open and read.

What has worked more effectively for me is to find other agents in the area who have similar properties for sale or lease, and target those specific agents with the listing. I create a brochure and then attach a handwritten note to the brochure. The handwritten note would explain that I knew they had a similar property for sale or lease, and if they find buyers or tenants who weren't satisfied with the agent's property, would he or she mind showing mine? This personal approach seems to net more showings for many of my listings.

# Broker's Open Houses

A broker's open house for commercial property is a marketing method in which you, as the listing agent, set aside a few hours and invite all the other commercial brokers in your marketplace to view and tour your listing. But do wine and cheese parties really work to attract other agents to look at your listings?

As with faxing and e-mailing brochures, the more realtors you can expose your listing to, the more likely you are to generate a buyer or tenant for the property. If you can get other agents to preview your listings, they're more likely to remember them when speaking with clients and hopefully will show the properties.

The truth, though, is that other agents generally don't care nearly as much about selling your listing as you do. So they are unlikely to show up for a broker's open house unless there is an alternate reason for being there. The best ways to attract other agents is to entice them through the use of food or door prizes. If an open house is scheduled during lunch hours, some agents will come for the free food. If you add a door prize, such as a dinner for two, you're likely to attract even more agents to your open house.

# Postcards

Postcards are inexpensive tools to get your message in front of potential customers. While I argued a few chapters back that postcards are not the way to attract and build a commercial real estate business, they may be a good marketing source for certain types of properties.

For example, if you are marketing a specific type of property that would appeal to owners of similar properties, such as a mini-mart, drycleaner, self-storage facility or gas station, a postcard may generate buyers who are looking to laterally expand their businesses.

Similarly, if you are selling an investment property in an area, you may want to send out an announcement of the listing by postcard to others who own similar investment properties. This type of marketing can work two ways. It may entice other investors to purchase your listing, but it is just as likely to produce other investors who may be considering selling and appreciate your aggressive approach to marketing.

When designing a postcard, like a brochure, be certain to determine who the most likely prospects are and focus the headline to speak directly to that group. If you are targeting several different groups with the same property, you may want to create different variations of the postcards with different headlines.

# Local Newspaper Advertising

Honestly, we get very little traction from advertising commercial properties in local newspapers unless the property is a multifamily investment property or a specific business for sale. Some investors prefer not to work with a specific realtor, believing they will find better deals on their own. These investors may search the newspapers, but buyers from newspaper advertising, in my experience, has been rare.

# Asking your clients for Referrals

Remember that your clients will become your leading source of referrals. Those referrals will become the lifeblood of your business, as long as you truly service your clients. The time when clients are most likely to notice other clients in need of your assistance and refer them is actually during the term of the listing and sale.

We all have a part of the brain called our reticular activator, which stimulates motivation. One of the functions of the reticular activator is to help us focus on things around us that are important to us. For example, when you first bought a new car, did you notice that same make, model and color almost everywhere? Did it seem like everyone went out and bought the exact same car as you the same day? The reticular activator is what was responsible for making you aware of other cars like yours. Pregnant women tend to notice pregnant women everywhere. And commercial property sellers tend to notice buyers and sellers of commercial property everywhere. Our goal is to turn that focus into referrals for our businesses.

Remember that our clients don't realize we need their help unless we ask for their help. During the listing presentation, I generally say something like "By the way, Mrs. Jones, I work primarily by referral. What that means is that unlike most agents, I'm going to dedicate a lot of time and effort in getting your property sold. What I hope you'll do for me in return is to refer me to any friends or relatives of yours who may also need assistance in buying or selling commercial real estate. I hope that I'll do such a good job for you that you'll enthusiastically refer me to people you know, because you won't want them to get stuck with bad-breath realty."

Telling a client once that you need referrals isn't enough. You have to strive to offer service that deserves referrals, and then you have to gently remind your clients often that you need their help. You can remind them during the process and you can remind them after you've closed while you're keeping in touch.

The beauty of referrals is that you can multiply your business. If you truly service your clients, and ask for referrals and remind them that's how you work, some will send you referrals consistently year after year. If you sold or leased 20 properties this year and each one refers you a client next year, that's 20 more clients. If you continue to generate your own business as well, you may do 40 transactions, and then 80. That's how you multiply business. While some clients won't send you any referrals at all, others will send you 2, 3, 5, or 10 next year.

One of my other suggestions is to remind your clients that you need their assistance by adding postscripts to your letters or emails "PS - Remember to keep me in mind when talking about buying or selling commercial real estate to your friends and family!" Or "Remember - I work primarily by referral - do you know of anyone thinking of buying or selling commercial real estate?"

And finally, start the process of maintaining contact with your clients after the sale. Send a newsletter, or better yet, try creating a system where you send something of value every month. Get sponsors to work with you to provide a free pizza, or a free hair cut, or something that highlights a business, but is a gift from you. No, I'm not asking you to pay for something. A salon pays between $50 and $100 to get a client in their chair the first time. They spend this on advertising in order to get the residual of the client coming back over and over again. Perhaps they'd be willing to give a free hair cut to your clients in return for the hope that they'll have a repeat customer.

Send out an endorsed letter from a salon that's willing to give each of your new transactions a free visit to the salon. You're giving a gift you're not paying for, and the salon is getting clients. Sounds like a win-win. Start the process of having events at least twice a year. Get your clients involved. Have fun, and build stronger bonds and friendships with your clients.

# Chapter 9:  Review Questions

1.  List 4 different Internet sites where commercial listings can be marketed:

    _____

    _____

    _____

    _____

2.  List 3 different items that should be included on flyers for Industrial properties:

    _____

    _____

    _____

3.  What is the most important information to include on a Raw Land brochure other than the location? _____

4.  True or False:  Feedback on showings is generally not necessary for commercial real estate sales.

5.  True or False:  Staging a property for sale or lease is not necessary since most buyers will renovate the property anyway.

# 10

# Working with Buyers

Working with Buyers can be challenging. Working with buyers can be frustrating. You will inevitably spend several days showing a buyer every single property you can find available, only to receive a phone call from them that they just found the perfect property and bought it from someone else. Of course, if it was easy to sell commercial properties all day long, we wouldn't be paid the big bucks, would we?

Unlike most property sellers, who are locked into a listing contract, buyers tend to be free agents, allowing them to purchase from anyone in the marketplace. Certainly, we can sign the buyer to a Relationship Agreement or Buyer's Agency Agreement. These contracts are both in our best interest and the client's best interest, but we have to carefully explain the benefits to potential clients without frightening them away.

Working on the buyer's or tenant's side of the transaction requires us to understand agency relationships, appropriately handle incoming calls, qualify both the ability of the buyer to purchase and the seriousness of the buyer, find the perfect property, handle buyer objections and negotiate a contract in their best interest.

Buyers may come to us as a result of seeing one of our signs on a property for sale, or an advertisement or a listing on the Internet. Our first buyers may actually be some of our existing property sellers or landlords. As you prospect to find property owners considering selling or leasing their commercial space, you will invariably run across owners who are looking to expand their holdings or move to larger space. These property owners are potential buyers as well. If you contact investors that own and lease out commercial space, these are also good prospective buyers.

# Agency Relationships

Agency is a legal term that describes the business relationship a Realtor, in this case, has with their client. Agents can represent a buyer or tenant in a transaction, or they can represent a seller or landlord in a transaction. In some states, agents can actually represent both in a limited fashion. Being an agent of the client, you have a fiduciary responsibility to work in your client's best interest at all times.

One aspect of agency that is confusing to new agents is that the real estate firm is considered to be one single agent. In court, you can't hire an attorney from a particular firm to argue with another attorney from the same firm, because the firm is considered to be one agent. Real estate brokerages follow the same laws. The duties of agents include:

- To represent the client's interests above their own interests.
- To exercise reasonable professional skill when representing their clients.
- To be loyal to the client's interests.
- To treat the client fairly and honestly.
- To disclose any potential conflicts of interest in a transaction.
- To advise the client to seek professional advice from others when the required knowledge is outside the scope of a real estate agent, such as accounting or engineering knowledge.

Although agency relationships change from state to state, the most common forms are:

- **Seller Agency** – The agent represents the seller's or landlord's interest in the transaction. In most cases, if a buyer or tenant contacts a seller's agent about a property, the agent <u>must</u> represent the best interest of the seller and may not represent the buyer in the transaction. A seller's agent should work to get the highest price possible on the property and the best terms for the seller.

- **Buyer Agency** – Similarly, as a Buyer's Agent, the agent represents the buyer's or tenant's interest in the transaction. The buyer's agent should work to get the lowest price possible on the property and the best terms for the buyer.

- **Dual Agency** – Because in most states, a caveat exists that allows an agency to designate one agent to represent the buyer and one to represent the seller, or allows a limited form of dual agency where the agent cannot give away either party's motivation or hurt the negotiating ability of either party.

# Handling Incoming Calls

Have you seen the movie "Field of Dreams"? Have a little faith. If you have listings, prospective buyers and tenants will come. This is an inventory business, so you must first master the art of prospecting for and listing commercial real estate. Once you've mastered listings, buyers and tenants will respond to the properties you are marketing.

As you place large commercial "for sale" and "for lease" signs along busy thoroughfares, potential buyers and tenants will call you. Some will call you simply out of curiosity, wanting to know the price. Others will be seriously looking for space to purchase or lease. Additional buyers and tenants will call from your listings on Internet sites like Loopnet or your company website, and still others will call from your advertising and marketing efforts. How you handle these incoming calls can make or break your real estate career.

The phone is the lifeblood of our industry. Whether we are making prospecting calls to obtain listing appointments, negotiating sales contracts or handling incoming buyer and tenant calls, we must make an effort to make every phone call count. Keep in mind that a single advertisement on your commercial listing in the Wall Street Journal may cost hundreds of dollars. That advertisement may only generate a call or two, so your skill at converting those calls to prospects can create a huge return on your advertising investment, or place a drain on your savings.

## Switching Properties

The honest truth that most agents don't want to reveal to their property sellers is that very few clients ever purchase or lease the property they initially call about. An advertisement or sign may attract the perfect buyer or tenant, who immediately purchases or leases the available space. This is rare, however. Most callers think the property is too high in price, smaller than they thought, or the wrong location.

Our goal with most advertising is to get prospective buyers and tenants to raise their hands and say *"Hey, I'm out here looking for a property"*. Once we identify a potential buyer or tenant, by their call to us, we can start directing our efforts to get them to work with us. Eventually, we'll have to find a way to meet with the client, qualify them, introduce them to the concept of buyer's agency and show them properties. First, we have to get over the initial objection that they don't want to see the property they are calling us about.

One method of accomplishing this task is by switching the caller to other properties that might be a better fit for the client. When you are advertising a property for sale, it pays to know the properties that are most likely competing with yours. Schedule some time to preview competing properties so that you have a clear picture of what else is available in the marketplace. Then, as callers ask about your property, you can intersperse questions about what would be the caller's perfect property, and lead into other properties on the market.

Caller: "Where is the advertised property located?"

Agent: "I'm just pulling up the details on that on my computer. I'll have it in a second. What area are you considering?"

Caller: "I'd like to stay in mid-Bucks County, preferably Doylestown or Perkasie, but I'd really like to be on Route 313 if possible."

Agent: "Route 313? How much were you looking to spend?"

Caller: "I'm not exactly sure. I don't want to be paying more than $2500 a month."

Agent: "That's fine. I have that property in front of me now. It's actually located close to Lansdale. Would that area work for you?"

Caller: "No, I'm sorry. That's too far for me."

Agent: "No problem. You mentioned you wanted to be close to Route 313. I remember a similar property that was for sale in that area. It's a really sharp looking office building, but it may be a bit higher in price than you'd like to go. Can I look that one up for you and call you back with the information?"

Caller: "Sure."

Agent: "Great. What's your phone number?"

Remember that one of your primary goals in the initial phone call is to obtain the client's name, phone number, and most importantly, their permission to call them back with more information. The Real estate sales industry is, in part, an information brokering business.

# Sign Calls

Commercial property signs are one of the best sources of buyer and tenant leads. When possible, I've used "Available" signs to attract both buyers and tenants. Some property owners request the sign to read "For Lease" or "For Lease Only" so the tenants aren't concerned about a property sale. However, generic commercial signs with your company's logo and the words "available" can attract a broader base of callers. Keep in mind that all property advertising is to attract potential buyers and tenants. These buyers or tenants may not want this particular property, but as you become skilled at switching buyers and tenants between properties, you're more likely to sell and lease your listings.

Buyers or tenants calling on a particular property are often surprised by the asking price. They obviously already know and like the location of the property, so the likely objections are either the asking price or the size of the space. In either case, your goal is to find out what price range the caller is comfortable with, or what size the caller requires.

Caller: "What is the asking price for the property on 5th and Broad?"

Agent: "Let me pull up the details on that property on my computer. I'll have it in a second. Are you looking to purchase or lease a property?"

Caller: "I'd like to buy."

Agent: "Is that the general location you'd like?"

Caller: "I'd like to stay close to I-78. I need access to the highway."

Agent: "I have that property on my screen now. They're currently asking $600,000. How much were you looking to spend?"

Caller: "Wow. That's high. I'm not looking for anything over $350,000."

Agent: "No problem. What type of building and what size are you looking to purchase?"

Caller: "Well, I need at least 2500 square feet."

Agent: "And you'd like something free standing, like the property on Broad?"

191

Client: "That's not necessary. I just need some visibility."

Agent: "Okay. I remember a similar property that was for sale in the area. I don't think it had a sign on it, because the owner didn't want anyone to know he's selling. Can I look that one up for you and call you back with the information?"

Caller: "That would be fine."

Agent: "Great. What's your phone number?"

An alternate approach to sign calls is to try to determine if the caller has written down several properties. Buyers or tenants looking for properties tend to drive through areas, and may write down the agency names and numbers on several properties for lease or sale. Rather than allow the prospect to call several other agents, who may pick them up as a potential client, you can research the same information for them.

Agent: "While you were driving around, did you see any other properties that interested you? They don't have to be listed by my firm."

Client: "I noticed a few."

Agent: "That's great. I can actually look them up for you now in our database. I can pull up all the information and let you know those prices as well. It's a bit easier than you calling through different agencies for information."

Caller: "I didn't realize you could do that."

Agent: "Definitely. Actually, we have a great software program at our company as well that helps us to find the perfect property. Each morning, the program searches all the new properties that came on the market in the last 24 hours by every agency in the system. It then emails you a copy of each of the new listings as they come on the market. This way, you know about properties before the big commercial sign even hits the lawn. The best listings sell quickly, often before a sign goes up."

Caller: "That sounds great."

Agent: "Well, let me pull up information on the other properties you drove by, and then we'll talk about your needs and try to get you into our Automatic Property Search program."

Incidentally, most agents have access to automatic search programs. Different MLS systems offer the service. Loopnet and other websites offer similar services. What differentiates you from the competition is that you're using it as a tool to convince buyers and tenants to work with you.

# Newspaper and Magazine Advertisement Calls

Prospective clients researching properties for sale in the newspaper or in magazines seldom know the exact address or location of the property being advertised. As Realtors, we do this in order to generate a call. Many of the callers will not be interested in the location of the property being advertised.

As with sign calls, these callers are probably not just considering one advertisement in the periodical. The likelihood is that they have circled several in the same newspaper or magazine. You can again ask them if they'd have interest in you pulling information on any other properties they may have circled.

Caller: "Where is the advertised property located?"

Agent: "I'm just pulling up the details on that on my computer. I'll have it in a second. What area are you considering?"

Caller: "I'd like to be close to the shore points. I'm particularly interested in property south of the turnpike."

Agent: "The shore points? That's my favorite area. How much were you looking to spend?"

Caller: "Probably no more than a million, unless it's a truly spectacular property."

Agent: "That's fine. I have that property in front of me now. It's actually located in Tapani, pretty far inland. I'm guessing that area wouldn't work for you?"

Caller: "No, I'm sorry. That's not where I'm looking to buy."

Agent: "You said you pulled this advertisement from the Morning News?"

Caller: "Yes."

Agent: "While you were looking through the ads, did any others stand out that might interest you? They don't have to be listed by my firm."

Client: "About 5 or 6."

Agent: "That's great. I can actually look them up for you now in our database. I can pull up all the information and let you know those prices as well. It's a bit easier than you calling through different agencies for information."

Caller: "Really?"

Agent: "Definitely. Actually, we have a great software program at our company as well that helps us to find the perfect property. Each morning, the program searches all the new properties that came on the market in the last 24 hours by every agency in the system. It then emails you a copy of each of the new listings as they come on the market. This way, you know about properties before the big commercial sign even hits the lawn. The best listings sell quickly, often before a sign goes up."

Caller: "That sounds great."

Agent: "Well, let me pull up information on the other properties you drove by, and then we'll talk about your needs and try to get you into our Automatic Property Search program."

## Internet Calls

Prospects calling from Internet advertising are generally more interested in the property than the typical sign call or newspaper ad call because they usually have more information about the property. Most commercial real estate sites on the Internet will display the general location of the property, the price and the size of the building. The primary objection for these calls is the specific location of the property.

# Follow Up, Follow Up, Follow Up

I met my wife at a party thrown by a friend of mine. After half an hour of conversation, I asked if she'd like to go out. She said "No". So I sent her flowers the next day. She called and said "Thanks for the flowers, but NO." So, naturally, I sent her flowers the day after. She called again and said "No *really* means no." So I sent flowers a third day in a row. This time she called and started with "This is getting close to stalking." I married her a year and a half later. Don't underestimate the power of follow up!

After receiving a buyer or tenant call, you now have a prospect who has identified themselves as someone considering buying or leasing a property. You've hopefully received some sort of permission to call back. Now you need to follow up regularly. The average commercial buyer speaks with between five and ten agents before purchasing. The agent who eventually sells a property to the prospect is often the agent who follows up most vigorously.

I'm not suggesting that you call the prospect every hour until they buy, but you need to maintain consistent contact. Part of that contact can be emailing or mailing listings of properties, but most of it should be actual telephone or physical contact. Sending listings to the prospect gives you a reason to call.

> Agent: "Hi, John? This is Malcolm at Greater Than Them Commercial Realty. I sent you some listings yesterday. I just wanted to make sure you received them."

> Client: "Yes, I did."

> Agent: "That's great. Sometimes our emails get caught in people's spam filters. I just wanted to make sure they came through. Have you had a chance to look through them yet?"

> Client: "No, not yet, but I saw the email."

> Agent: "Okay. I'll check back with you in a day or so. Let me know if any of the properties look interesting enough that you'd like to tour them."

> Client: "I will."

Our buyer specialists keep in touch by setting aside one afternoon a week to call through all of their prospects. Buyers or tenants who are actively searching for property may need to be called daily. You'll have to make a judgment call on each prospect.

I suggest separating your buyers into categories, such as A, B and C. "A" buyers may be buyers, investors or tenants who are qualified and need to move on a property within 30 to 90 days. "B" buyers may be qualified and want to move, but not have a specific time frame. "C" buyers would be everybody else.

# Alternate places to find buyers

Buyers and investors are everywhere. You simply need to try to identify them and then follow up. So far, we've discussed passive methods of attracting buyers using signs and advertising. You can also get potential purchasers to let you know they have some interest in investing in real estate by offering free information or free workshops.

As we described in the prospecting system for listings, workshops can be very effective in bringing clients to you and setting yourself apart as the expert in the field. Some suggestions of potential target audiences for your business are:

- **Turning Home Equity into Investment Capital** – As home owners pay down their mortgage, and the home value appreciates, the owner's equity position in the property grows. This equity can be tapped into as a possible down payment on an investment property.

- **Retirement or College Planning Using Real Estate** – This workshop has been very effective for my team. Many young couples are concerned about their ability to provide college education to their children. Others are concerned about retirement. Real Estate is a very effective investment plan for these groups. Work with a mortgage broker and build a workshop around the concept of using Real Estate investments as a strategy.

Another method may be to advertise a free informative booklet on *"How to use Real Estate to fund your retirement"* or *"How to pay for your child's college tuition using Real Estate"*. Your goal, again, is to get potential buyers raising their hands to say "I'm interested in possibly buying." Once you accomplish that, you can follow up, or you can schedule a workshop to show the customers the process of investing, step by step.

# Explaining Buyer Agency

Most commercial buyers and investors want to shop on their own for a property for two reasons. First, they don't want to be locked into a contract and ultimately find themselves unhappy with their representation. Secondly, they feel that they have the best chance of finding a property if they speak with ten or twenty Realtors. Why? Because they don't understand that most agents have access to all the same properties through the MLS, Loopnet and commercial databases.

What these buyers and investors fail to understand is that if they *don't* sign with an agent to exclusively represent them, they are actually less likely to find the perfect property. Let's consider the issue from the agent's perspective. If you have twenty investors that call you, and two of them are willing to sign buyer agency contracts with you, who are you going to spend most of your time working to service? Will you, as a Realtor, run around town trying to get the best deals with clients that are not loyal to you, or concentrate on those buyers who have selected you to represent them?

So we need to explain to buyers and investors that they are *more* likely to find out about every property for sale if they utilize the services of a buyer representative, and sign a buyer agency agreement. If not, they'll have fifteen agents ignoring them and five more half-heartedly sending them listings every once in a while. The same is true of tenant representation. An agent will be far more likely to put work into finding the best lease deals if the agent is assured that he or she will get paid once a buyer purchases or a tenant leases a property.

# The Buyer Presentation

Buyer presentations are often less formal than seller presentations, but are still critically important. Without a specific presentation outlining what you do for a buyer, you will have a difficult time explaining to a buyer why they should sign a buyer agency contract with you, and why they should contact you about every property they want to view.

If you diligently call the prospect after your initial contact and mail or email them listings, you are more likely to get them to meet with you in person. I suggest that you attempt to get the potential buyer or tenant back to your office in order to sit down at a table and explain the buying or leasing process and how you can assist the client. You may be able to do this by telling the buyer or tenant that you'd like to look through different commercial database systems with them in order to get a better idea of what they're looking to purchase or lease. You may have to show the buyer a property or two

197

before you can get them to the office. Worst case, you should at least sit down with the prospect at a diner or restaurant so you can visually show them how you work.

Just as with a listing presentation, a visual presentation is far more effective in helping the buyer or tenant to understand your value as a buyer's representative or buyer's agent. You may start the conversation with "John and Sally, if you have a couple minutes, I'd like to give you a brief explanation of how the process works in finding you the perfect property and moving forward to purchase or lease it, and also briefly explain what I do in order to assist you in finding the perfect property. Would that be okay?"

Once again, our younger agents prefer to open a laptop and run through a brief PowerPoint presentation. I prefer a 3-ring binder with lots of colorful examples. Either way, your presentation should *show* the prospect why they should work with you rather than *tell* them. The presentation should be designed to show the prospect that you are on their side, and that your focus is on their needs.

The presentation should be broken into three major components. The first is an explanation of buyer's agency. The second section of the presentation should be an outline of your duties and how you find properties. The last section should include a flow chart and an explanation of the process of buying or leasing commercial property.

## 1st Section: Buyer Agency

- What *is* Buyer Agency?
- Why most agents won't spend a lot of time assisting clients who aren't represented by them.
- If you call the Listing Agent, you're calling the person who represents the best interests of the Seller or Landlord. Get someone on *your* side.
- Buyer Agency costs the buyer *nothing*.

## 2nd Section: Your Agent's Responsibilities

- Your agent will assist you in finding the best property to suit your needs.
- Your agent will use their exclusive Automatic Search Program to assist you in finding the best properties.
- Your agent will negotiate the lowest price for you.
- Your agent will assist you in securing the best financing available for your situation.
- Your agent will make the transaction as painless and worry free as possible.
- All of your agent's services are free (unless you charge for services).

**3<sup>rd</sup> Section:  The Process of Buying or Leasing Commercial Property**

- Include a flow chart of the process and then break down the process on individual pages.
- Being qualified by a commercial mortgage broker early in the process is important.
- The Search for properties.
- Writing a "Letter of Intent" on a property.
- Negotiating a Sale or Lease in your best interest.
- Completing a final Agreement of Sale or Lease.
- What are property inspections?
- Zoning, Environmental and other conditions.
- Ordering Title Insurance and Scheduling Settlement.

# Pre-Qualification / Pre-Approval

If the prospect is a buyer or investor, your next step in the buyer process is to attempt to have the buyer meet with a commercial mortgage broker or loan officer.  If you don't have your buyers pre-qualified or pre-approved for a mortgage, you'll discover, after showing them 27 properties and wasting 8 days with them, that they don't qualify for a commercial loan.  As a matter of fact, they will probably *never* qualify for a commercial loan.  And they seemed like such nice people, too.

Another benefit of meeting with a loan officer early in the process is that we can often catch mortgage issues early and try to correct them before writing an offer on a property.  For example, a buyer may have credit issues that can be corrected, or credit on their credit report that isn't even theirs.  You won't know until it's checked.

# Handling Buyer and Tenant Objections

As with seller objections, when you hear a buyer objection, try not to take an immediate defensive stance.  Our goal, again, is to educate our prospect or client to help them make good decisions.  The way to handle buyer objections is a little different than seller objections, because buyer objections may actually be buying signs.  A buyer feels the need to complain about a property in order to justify their outrageously low offer price.  It is almost an art form trying to distinguish real objections from fictitious ones.

Listen carefully to the objection. Repeat the objection, and then ask a question to try to determine if the objection is real. For example, if a buyer tells you that they like the location and the size, but the property won't work for them because the layout is all wrong. You can repeat the objection, and then ask if they'd consider the property if the owner reconfigured the property to meet the buyer's needs.

**Lease Example**:

Our goal is to determine if the objection is real or if it's a signal that they like the property and would accept it, if it were changed.

> Client: "I like the location and the size, but this property won't work for me. The layout is terrible for a dental office."
>
> Agent: "The layout's not good?"
>
> Client: "No. I need a nice lobby area and then larger offices than what's existing now."
>
> Agent: "I understand. That will help me to search for other properties for you, now that I understand that need. I have a thought though. Sometimes landlords are willing to renovate or reconfigure a property to meet the tenant's needs. That would likely add to the monthly rental rate, but I could certainly ask the owner. Since the location and size are right, would you consider the property if it were reconfigured to your specifications?"

**Purchase Example:**

> Client: "I like the location and the size, but this property won't work for me. The layout is terrible for a dental office."
>
> Agent: "The layout's not good?"
>
> Client: "No. I need a nice lobby area and then larger offices than what's existing now."
>
> Agent: "I understand. That will help me to search for other properties for you, now that I understand that need. I have a thought though. We can often build reconstruction of a property into the mortgage for the property. I could probably get an estimate within a few days to see what

it would cost to reconfigure the property to your specifications. Since the location and size are right, would you consider the property if it were reconfigured to your specifications?"

Client: "I guess it would depend on the cost."

Agent: "Why don't we go back through the property and you can lay out a rough idea of how it would look if it were perfect. I will get an estimate from one of our contractors, and we'll see how much that would add to your monthly mortgage payment."

## Summary

Understanding how to work with buyers and tenants is a critical component in selling and leasing commercial real estate. Buyers are attracted to properties through signs, printed advertising, and Internet advertising. Buyers seldom purchase the property they initially call about. Handling incoming calls properly includes possibly switching the caller to other properties, and then obtaining permission from the caller to contact them with more information. Once an agent has received permission to call back, the agent needs to follow up regularly and attempt to secure a meeting with the client.

When meeting with a buyer or tenant, the agent should spend time explaining the benefits of buyer agency, and outline the agent's responsibility to the buyer. The next steps are qualifying the buyer for a loan, and beginning the process of site selection with the buyer or tenant. Once the "right" property is found, the agent must handle the buyer's objections, and prepare an offer for purchase or lease.

# Chapter 10: Review Questions

1.	Representing a client's interests above your own is one of the aspects of Buyer Agency.  List 3 other aspects:

	_____
	_____
	_____

2.	True or False:  In most states, a caveat exists that allows an agency to designate one agent to represent the buyer and one to represent the seller, or allows a limited form of dual agency.  In this form of dual agency, an agent is generally allowed to disclose the seller's primary reason for selling the property.

3.	True or False:  When a prospect calls an agent about a property, the agent must talk exclusively about that property, because they are representing the interest of the seller.

4.	True or False:  Signs should always indicate whether the property is for sale or for lease, so that clients will not be confused.

5.	True or False:  When handling advertising calls, an agent may not answer questions about advertisements of other brokers.

# 11

# The Sale

The sale is the culmination of all your hard work marketing a listing or showing properties to buyers. Like every other aspect of commercial real estate, the sale is a process composed of several stages. The offer and negotiation are the first phase of a successful real estate transaction. The second phase is the inspection and mortgage phase. During this period, property inspections are completed, zoning applications are made and the buyer applies for their mortgage. The final phase is title insurance and settlement.

As a professional Realtor, part of your responsibility is to guide your client or clients through the hazards of the sales process. Typically a Realtor writes the initial offer to purchase, offer to lease or letter of intent to purchase or lease. The Realtor then negotiates the offer in the best interest of his or her clients. The final agreement of sale may be constructed by an attorney or may be done by a Realtor.

Although the choice of attorneys, inspectors, engineers, surveyors, loan companies and title insurance companies are up to the purchaser of the property, a Realtor is often called upon to give

## Steps to a Sale

1. Offer is written and presented.

2. Offer is negotiated.

3. Final Sales Contract is executed.

4. Due Diligence Period may begin (if part of agreement).

5. Inspections are performed on the property.

6. Inspection results are negotiated.

7. Buyer applies for a mortgage.

8. Title Insurance is ordered.

9. Settlement is scheduled.

10. Final settlement.

advice or thoughts on hiring good and reputable firms. Please check your state laws, however, to avoid steering the buyers. The Realtor next has to facilitate any inspections, surveys, mortgages and title work and co-ordinate information between all parties. An agent must keep their buyers and sellers informed during each step of the process. If all goes well, a Realtor may schedule a settlement date with an attorney or title company and co-ordinate the buyer, seller, lender and any co-operating agent to meet for settlement.

Unfortunately, a sale can come unhinged at any point during the transaction. Agents have a habit of calculating, and often spending, their commission before settlement occurs. Please don't count your commissions until after final settlement. Regardless of how skilled and knowledgeable you are as a Realtor, some sales will not close. Whether they fall apart because of inspection results, zoning issues, financing problems or one party gets cold feet, not all settle.

## Broker Co-Operation Agreement

Some brokers will not pay a co-operating fee for a buyer. These brokers tell Buyer's Agents to "Go get the fee from your own client". This attitude usually comes back to haunt these broker's in the long run. Any quick fee a broker makes by injuring another Realtor or broker is eventually lost several times.

However, prior to showing the property or writing the offer, an agent should verify they will be paid on the transaction. If the property is listed in a Multiple Listing System, the Board of Realtors typically protects commissions advertised. If the commercial broker is not a member of the MLS, then you should obtain a Broker Co-Operation Agreement from that broker, prior to the offer, outlining what you are to be paid for bringing a buyer and how it is to be paid.

## Letter of Intent

In many areas across the country, a Letter of Intent is a common practice before writing a full Sales Contract. A Letter of Intent spells out the basic terms of an offer. These simple forms are often used in order to determine whether or not the property owner will consider selling or leasing the property at the price and terms of the Letter, without spending the time and money to have a full Sales Contract drafted.

A Letter of Intent should spell out the buyer's or tenant's names, the owner's name, a property description, all offering terms including price, inspections and settlement date, and signatures of all parties. A sample Letter of Intent is displayed on the next page.

# Letter of Intent

September 2, 2008

Tom Sullivan
Creative Commercial Realty
151 55<sup>th</sup> Avenue, Suite 302
New York, NY 01001

Re: 37 North Ridge Avenue, New York


Dear Mr. Sullivan:

This letter of intent shall set forth the terms of our proposed purchase agreement, to which terms the parties shall be bound upon the execution and delivery of a lease agreement. The parties shall work together in good faith to consummate an Agreement of Sale on the terms set forth herein. For the purposes of this letter of intent, "Seller" shall be Alex Martin and Company, Inc and "Buyer" shall be Fruit for Less, Inc.

Premises: 37 North Ridge Avenue, New York, better described as tax parcel 11-527-36-1

Purchase Price: Nine Hundred Fifty Thousand Dollars ($950,000.00)

Settlement Date: Settlement shall take place on or before November 5, 2008.

Mortgage: The agreement of sale shall be contingent upon buyer's securing a mortgage for Six Hundred Seventy Five Thousand Dollars ($675,000.00)

Contingencies:

The agreement of sale shall be contingent upon a zoning approval for a retail fruit market within 45 days of execution of agreement of sale.

The agreement of sale shall be contingent upon acceptable results from a building inspection and engineering inspection within 20 days of execution of agreement of sale.

Deposit: Buyer will provide a deposit on the property of Twenty Thousand Dollars ($20,000.00)

Sincerely,

Loren Keim
Century 21 Keim Commercial Realtors


Buyer: _____     Seller: _____
Buyer: _____     Seller: _____
Buyer: _____     Seller: _____

# Negotiating

There are full classes on negotiation techniques. As you begin your career as a real estate professional, you'll have to feel your way through negotiations. Most sales or leases require some give and take between the owner and the buyer or tenant. Negotiating on your client's behalf can also be something of an art form. When you present a counter offer to your buyer or tenant, your tone of voice, inflection and attitude may impact your buyer's reaction.

For example, a buyer offers $500,000 on a property listed at $600,000. If you are the agent representing the seller and you react with "I can't *believe* this offer, Mr. Seller! $100,000 off the price? What *was* he thinking?" You'll probably never get the sale to closing because the seller will be likely not counter, taking offense to the initial offer. The truth is that the buyer, in many cases, has emotionally purchased the property and may come up to a reasonable price. A better approach might be "Well, don't be offended, but I have an initial offer for you on your property. The buyer, like everyone, is making a low offer to see what you're willing to do. Please don't be offended. Let's talk about our counter offer options."

The same is true when dealing with buyers. If you are presenting a counter offer from the seller of $550,000 and tell the buyer "You'll never believe this counter offer", you're again unlikely to get the buyer and seller closer together. Remember that you must represent the best interest of your client, but the best interest of your client may also be to acquire the property. Ultimately, all decisions are made by the buyer and seller. However, you'll have to make a judgment call on whether it is in the best interest of your client that you advise them to hold firm on their offer, or to try to carefully bring the buyer and seller closer together.

Offers and counter offers should be in writing to avoid misunderstandings. Although price is the most common negotiating point, almost anything in an agreement may be negotiated. The date of possession, the terms of the agreement, deposit amount and improvements or inspections are all fair game for negotiations.

# Due Diligence Periods

In my experience, most commercial sales allow the buyer a period of time to study or investigate the property and the property's financial information. If the buyer discovers something amiss during this study period, the buyer may withdraw from purchasing the property and have their deposit monies returned. This period of time is referred to as a **due diligence period** and generally lasts between 15 and 45 days for office, retail, shopping center, hospitality and multi family property purchases. Raw land purchases may have a longer due diligence period to allow the purchaser to present a sketch plan of the proposed use to the local municipality, perform percolation testing for sewage and soil testing. Industrial property purchases may also have lengthier due diligence periods in order to study the soils and possible contaminants.

After the expiration of the due diligence period, the buyer generally must proceed with the sale or risk losing their deposit monies. Inspections performed during the due diligence phase of the agreement can include physical or structural inspection, water testing, and environmental testing. Studies performed during the period can include inspections of all documents pertaining to the business or income and expenses including all leases, income tax returns, ledgers, profit and loss statements and similar documents. Other work done during a due diligence period can include preliminary zoning approvals, zoning verifications or percolation tests to determine suitability for on-site sewage systems.

## Property and Building Inspections

Building inspections are done to insure the buyer does not walk into any "surprises" after settlement. A typical building inspection will consist of 2 parts. The first part is a full system and structural inspection. The second is an inspection to verify compliance with municipal, state and federal laws and regulations with regard to the physical building and property.

A full system and structural inspection can take hours or days to complete, and may cost the buyer between several hundred and several thousand dollars depending on the size of the building and the extent of the inspections. Typical system inspections assess the condition of the electrical system, plumbing system, and heating and air conditioning systems. The structural component of the inspection will assess the physical condition of the buildings, including the roof, foundation, structural integrity, water penetration, insect infiltration, and similar potential issues. The structural component will also examine issues affecting the property including drainage, potential run-off issues, and similar issues. Other parts of the inspection might include drinking water quality and sewage system inspections if the property is serviced by an on-site sewage system.

The compliance part of a full building inspection may include analysis of any potential municipal code violations, adequacy of the fire protection system or alarm system, compliance with the Americans with Disabilities Act (ADA), and any other compliance issues that may exist. Although many municipalities create their own compliance standards, the primary standard for compliance is the Building Officials and Code Administrators (BOCA) guide.

Each of these inspections is done to protect the interest of the buyer, and to help limit their exposure to hidden property defects. For example, an inspection may reveal a roof that has only months of life left, and a lack of required handicapped bathrooms, which may require significant reconfiguration of the space at a substantial cost. If something significantly wrong is discovered during the inspection phase, the buyer can either renegotiate the transaction or cancel the transaction. Certainly a buyer could also proceed forward with the transaction, if they still want the property, but they'll proceed with knowledge of the potential pitfalls of the property.

## Environmental Testing

Depending on the type of property being purchased, environmental testing is actually a requirement of many lenders. Environmental inspections can include soil testing for contamination, fuel tank integrity, flood plain or wetlands delineation and similar tests. The typical test that is ordered is a "Phase 1" study, also known as an Environmental Assessment Report. Phase 1 studies typically also research any other properties within ½ mile that are known to have contamination.

If a Phase 1 study finds an issue, the purchaser can either withdraw from the property, or negotiate to have a Phase II study done, which is more extensive and more expensive. A Phase II study may include test borings in the ground and full analysis.

## Verifying the Income and Expenses

Any financial records a purchaser would like to review should be spelled out clearly in a Sales Contract. With an investment property, such as a multi family property or office building, the buyer will request any information backing up the income and expenses. Typically, this includes tax returns, an accountant's profit and loss statement, records of rent payments, and copies of all bills on the property including utilities, maintenance bills and tax bills. The purchaser can then have their own financial advisor or accountant pour over the records to determine the accuracy of the income and expense numbers that were most likely provided prior to an offer.

Additionally, a purchaser should request copies of all leases so that the rental rate, lease terms, and length of lease can be matched against any previously provided documentation. Records of rental payment history will also show any slow paying tenants or tenants who are behind on their payments.

In the event that your client is purchasing a business, all receipts for the prior three years may be requested for your client's review.

## Zoning Verification or Zoning Approvals

As a buyer's representative, it is extremely important that you assist the buyer in verification that the property can be utilized for the buyer's purposes. Some uses may simply require verification that the use is acceptable and obtain a permit for the use. Other uses may require a full zoning appeal and hearing. Hearings may require surveys, engineering studies, topography studies and notification of any adjacent property owners of your client's intention to change the use of the property.

Depending on the type of property and the location, zoning approvals may take months. If the property is a land parcel in subdivision, the approvals could potentially take years. Before preparing a formal Sales Contract, an agent should always contact the municipality's zoning office or planning commission to determine how long the process may take and what the process may involve. Even if the zoning or planning officers can give you specific instructions, you should always give the buyer the option of contacting an attorney who is familiar with the zoning process in that location.

## Negotiating Repairs

Inspections and verifications during a due diligence period can often lead to additional negotiating on the property. Negotiations may entail requesting the seller to repair or correct defects discovered by the inspectors. Sellers seldom correct all defects found by inspectors, so an agent may have to prepare his or her buyer to consider what defects concern them the most.

Other negotiating may entail a possible reduction in the price of the property to cover repairs or a reduction because the income and expense figures are found to be incorrect, lessening the return on the property.

# Parts of a Sales Contract

A sales contract for Real Property must be in writing in order to be valid. The sales contract is a legal contract between the owner of the property and the purchaser. In most areas, standard sales contract forms for commercial real estate are available from either the local association of realtors or the state association of realtors. However, due to the nature of commercial real estate, many agreements are prepared by attorneys.

As with any previous contract, including leases and listing contracts, there are certain elements that must be included to create something that is both legal and binding on both parties.

1.   **Name of all Parties** – The owners(s) of the property and the purchaser(s) of the property.

---
Owner(s) / Seller(s) of Property: _____

Buyer(s) / Purchaser(s) of Property: _____

---

2.   **Description of Property** – Address, tax parcel information and a description of the property in order to avoid any confusion.

---
Seller agrees to convey to Buyer, who hereby agrees to purchase all that certain lot with buildings and improvements erected thereon, as described in the following property description:

**PROPERTY DESCRIPTION:**

Address _____

Municipality (city, borough, township) _____

County _____ School District _____

Zoning _____ Present Use _____

Property Identification -Tax ID#; Parcel #; Lot, Block; Deed Book, Page, Recording Date)

_____

---

3.   **Purchase Price** – The price the buyer is willing to pay for the property.

---
**PURCHASE PRICE:**

Purchase Price _____ which will be paid to

Seller by Buyer as follows:

    Cash or check at signing this Agreement:         $_____

    Cash or check within ____ days of the execution of this Agreement:

                                                  $_____

    Cash or cashier's check at time of settlement:     $_____

    Total:                                            $_____

---

4.   **Settlement Date** – Date of settlement:

---
**SETTLEMENT DATE:**

Settlement shall be on or before _____

---

210

5. **Fixtures, Equipment, Inventory and Personal Property Remaining With Property** – What items will be included with the sale, including any fixtures, equipment, inventory or personal property.

---

**FIXTURES, EQUIPMENT, INVENTORY, PERSONAL PROPERTY:**

Included in the sale are all permanently installed fixtures in the property and any fixtures, equipment, inventory or personal property itemized below:

---

6. **Time is of the Essence**

---

**DATES / TIME IS OF THE ESSENCE:**

The settlement date and all other dates and times referred to for the performance of any of the obligations of this Agreement are of the essence and are binding.

---

7. **Good Title to the Property** – The seller should guarantee that the property will be delivered free and clear of any outstanding liens and with good and marketable title.

---

**GOOD AND MARKETABLE TITLE:**

The property shall be conveyed with good and marketable title as is insurable by a reputable title insurance company, free and clear of all liens, encumbrances, and easement, excepting: existing deed restrictions; historic preservation restrictions or ordinances; building restrictions; ordinances; easements of roads; easements visible upon the ground; easements of record; and privileges or rights of public service companies, if any.

---

8. **Property Possession** – Will the buyer take possession at the time of settlement, and in what condition will the property be conveyed to the buyer?

---

**PROPERTY POSSESSION:**

Possession is to be delivered to buyer by deed, keys and physical possession. Seller shall deliver the property free of debris, with all structures broom-clean, at day and time of settlement, and / or assign any existing lease(s) to the buyer, together with any security deposits and interest, at day and time of settlement, if property is leased at the execution of this Agreement.

# Contingency Clauses for a Sales Contract

There are literally dozens, if not hundreds, of potential contingencies that can be added to a contract. Some contingencies are specific to types of properties or to specific areas of the country. The most common contingencies in Commercial Sales Contracts include:

- **Mortgage Contingency** – Make sure the buyer has an escape clause to the Sales Contract if they are unable to obtain a mortgage. Although it is negotiable, typically the buyer would receive their deposit money back if the mortgage is denied.

---

**MORTGAGE CONTINGENCY:**

___ The Agreement of Sale is not contingent on mortgage financing.
___ The Agreement of Sale is contingent upon Buyer obtaining mortgaging financing as outlined below:

_____ First Mortgage on the Property in the Amount of $_____ for a term of _____ Years.
Type of Mortgage _____
_____ Second Mortgage on the Property in the Amount of $_____ for a term of _____ Years.
Type of Mortgage _____

Mortgage commitment date: _____. If Buyer cannot provide a copy of a mortgage by the commitment date

Seller does not receive a copy of Buyer's mortgage commitment(s) by this date. Buyer and Seller agree to extend the mortgage commitment date until Seller terminates this Agreement by written notice to Buyer.

---

- **Property Inspection Contingency** – This contingency is to allow the buyer to conduct inspections of the property including structural, engineering, water, sewer, and any systems such as the heating, plumbing, or electrical.

---

**PROPERTY INSPECTION CONTINGENCY:**

Buyer has the option to conduct property inspections, certifications and/or investigations. Buyer, at Buyer's expense, may have inspections, certifications and/or investigations completed by properly licensed or otherwise qualified professionals.

---

- **Zoning Verification Contingency** – As outlined in the previous section, an agent must protect their client by assisting in the verification that the property can be utilized for the buyer's purposes. Some uses may simply require verification that the use is acceptable and obtain a permit for the use. Other uses may require a full zoning appeal and hearing. For a simple verification, a clause such as the following may suffice:

---

**ZONING VERIFICATION CONTINGENCY:**

Buyer may, at buyer's expense, verify the proposed or current use of the Property as \_\_\_\_\_ _____ is permitted under the current zoning regulations for the Property. This verification, and any required permits for the proposed use, must be completed within 15 days of the execution of the Agreement of Sale.

Should buyer be unable to verify the use as permitted or be unable to obtain the permits necessary for the use, the buyer must:

(A)  Accept the property "As Is" and proceed with the purchase OR
(B)  Terminate the Agreement of Sale by written notice to the Seller, and the Seller shall return all deposit monies to the Buyer.

---

- **Zoning Approval Contingency** – If the buyer's proposed use of the property requires approval by a zoning board or planning commission, a clause should be added to the sales contract to protect the buyer's interest if the use is not permitted.

---

**ZONING APPROVAL CONTINGENCY:**

Buyer will make a formal written application of zoning approval, variance, non-conforming use, or special exception from _____ to use the Property as _____ within 10 Days of the execution of the Agreement of Sale,.

Buyer will pay for all costs associates with the application and approval process including required municipality application fees, review fees, legal representation, engineering or surveying fees, or any other similar costs.

If final approval for the use is not obtained by _____, Buyer will:
(A)  Accept the Property with the current zoning OR
(B)  Terminate the Agreement of Sale by written notice to Seller, with all deposit monies returned to Buyer according to the terms of the Agreement of Sale.

---

- **Review of Leases Contingency** – A condition of the agreement that allows the purchaser a period of time to review the leases for any unexpected issues.

---

**LEASE REVIEW CONTINGENCY:**

Seller will furnish to buyer, within 10 days of the Execution Date of the Agreement of Sale, copies of all written lease agreements currently in effect, tenant notices or correspondence, and a written explanation of the terms of any oral leases for the property.

Buyer will have 5 days to review all leases and documents upon receipt from Seller. Buyer will then:
(A)   Accept the Property OR
(B)   Terminate the Agreement of Sale by written notice to Seller, with all deposit monies returned to Buyer

---

- **Lease Assignment and Security Deposit Clause** – The Seller should assign all leases to the Buyer at time of settlement and deliver any security deposits and interest for those deposits.

---

**LEASE ASSIGNMENTS AND SECURITY DEPOSITS:**

Seller will assign all leases and security deposits, together with the interest, if any, to Buyer at time of settlement.

---

# Title Insurance

Title insurance is an insurance policy that can protect the buyer and the lender from losses that arise from errors or fraud in the chain of title to the real property being conveyed. Title insurance also guarantees that any current mortgages or liens against the property have been paid off at settlement, and will cover the cost of any mortgages or liens discovered after the buyer take's ownership that may not have been properly satisfied.

Property deeds in the United States can actually go back hundreds of years, depending on where in the country the property is located. In that period of time, there have been changes in ownership. If, at some point in the past, a signature to transfer the title was missed, or fraud was committed in transferring the title, or a mortgage was placed on the property and never properly satisfied, someone else may have some interest in the property.

All deeds are recorded in a central county or jurisdictional government recording office where the property is located, such as a "County Recorder of Deeds". These records are public information and can be viewed by anyone. A title insurance company conducts a process called a **title search** to examine the deeds or title to the property. Title searches also check with any government office or recording office where liens may be filed against the property including tax liens, mortgages, judgments, easements or any other encumbrance. Typical offices investigated include the local Courthouse, the Recorder of Deeds Office, the Prothonotary's Office, with all taxing authorities and anywhere else a lien or defect in title may exist. Once the title search is completed, a title insurance policy is issued to the buyer and the mortgage company to insure for any claims and legal fees.

Title Insurance can be purchased from Title Insurance companies or from attorneys. Some states require an attorney handle the settlement process. This type of insurance is paid in one lump sum at the time of settlement. Depending on the area of the country, either buyers or sellers may pay for the insurance.

Title insurance is required by banks and lenders to protect their interest in the property. Lenders typically ask for insurance in an amount equal to the loan. The lender's policy only insures any loss by the lender. For a small additional fee, a buyer can purchase an owner's policy in addition to the lender's policy to cover the full value of the property. A third type of title insurance, called extended owner's coverage, protects the purchaser from prior violations of covenants or building permit violations.

## Types of Title Insurance Coverage:

- **Lender's Title Policy Coverage** – Covers the lender up to an amount equal to the loan against any previously recorded mortgages, mechanic's liens, unrecorded liens, unrecorded easements and other defects in title. The lender's policy amount declines as the loan balance declines. Lender's policies are also assignable to a lender who may purchase the mortgage.

- **Owner's Title Policy Coverage** – Covers the owner for the value of the property against unsatisfied mortgages or liens during a prior ownership, incorrect or forged signatures, lack of competency, defective recording, fraud and lack of a right of access. The owner's policy guarantees clear title, but is not assignable to other parties.

- **Extended Owner's Coverage** – Covers the owner for errors stemming from subdivision maps, incorrect surveys, claims for adverse possession (when a neighbor claims they have used the property for a significant period of time and now "own" it), buildings encroaching on a neighboring property, off-record liens (such as unrecorded mechanic's liens or estate tax liens), pre-existing violations of zoning ordinances.

Unlike most insurance, owner's title insurance protection lasts for the entire term of ownership. The term of ownership includes the owner and their heirs. However, the insurance protects solely against losses from events that occurred prior to the date the insurance was issued.

# Settlement

Settlement, also known as Closing, is the end of the process of purchasing a property. In most cases, at settlement, the property seller receives their proceeds check, and the buyer receives the keys, the deed and possession of the property they are purchasing. During the course of settlement, the buyer signs all the necessary loan documentation and the buyer and seller sign a plethora of paperwork.

Settlement may be attended by the buyer, the seller, the agent's representing both parties, a loan officer, attorneys representing either party, a settlement agent, who may be an attorney, a title insurance representative or an escrow agent, depending on the region of the country in which the transaction takes place.

Practices and customs vary from area to area for settlement, but all settlements involve a settlement statement which itemizes all fees paid by the buyer and all fees paid by the seller. In most jurisdictions, the settlement agent collects one check from the buyer and delivers checks to the seller, the current mortgage lender, the Realtors and any other parties that must be paid out of the transaction. Most settlement agents require the buyer to provide certified funds at time of settlement.

# Summary

The sale begins with an offer to purchase. This offer may be in the form of a formal Sales Contract or it may be in the form of a Letter of Intent. The offer is negotiated between the parties and if successful, a final Sales Contract is written and signed by all parties.

After a final Sales Contract is signed, the buyer generally performs a due diligence on the property in the form of physical and environmental inspections of the property, verification of zoning or applications for approval of the buyer's use, and review of all financial documentation and leases of the property. If the inspections, zoning and financial documentation meet with the buyer's approval, the buyer proceeds with the sale, finalizing the mortgage application and purchasing title insurance.

The mortgage company will require an appraisal of the property to verify the value, and may require additional inspections of the property including engineering or environmental. Once the mortgage approval is received, settlement may be scheduled. Settlement is the final culmination of the purchasing process and involves the buyer paying the remainder of the purchase price to the seller, and the seller turning the property over to the buyer.

# Chapter 11: Review Questions

1. List 3 things a buyer may elect to do during a due diligence period:

   _____
   _____
   _____

2. True or False: Environmental inspections are often a requirement of the lender for the property.

3. True or False: Broker co-operating agreements are generally not necessary because the Board of Realtors always protects a Realtor's commissions.

4. True or False: Building inspections are generally limited to the primary structure on the property. Additional inspections require a separate inspector.

5. BOCA stands for:

   A. Building and Occupational Code Authority
   B. Building and Occupational Code Administrators
   C. Building Officials and Code Administrators
   D. Building Officials and Code Authority

6. True or False: Zoning verifications are generally unnecessary if the buyer is planning to use the property for the exact same use as the prior owner.

7. True or False: A Sales Agreement must be in writing to be enforceable.

8. True or False: Title Insurance is generally required by most lenders.

9. A Standard Owner's Policy for Title Insurance covers all of the following except:

   A. Forged documents.
   B. Documents signed by incompetent individuals.
   C. Missed prior mortgages that were not satisfied.
   D. Lack of a right to access the property.
   E. Unrecorded mechanic's liens.

# Appendix A - Depreciation and Cost Recovery Charts

Depreciation of a real estate asset is the act of recovering the cost of an income producing property by deducting a portion of that cost yearly on your tax return. Only the portion of property used for income or rental purposes can be depreciated. There are three primary factors in determining how much an investor can deduct from their taxes.

1. The investor's basis in the property (usually the original purchase price of the property)
2. The recovery period for the type of property (Residential Rental Property, Non-Residential Rental Property, Land Improvements and Personal Property)
3. The method of depreciation used.

A property may be depreciated on taxes if the property meets all the following requirements:

1. The property may only be depreciated by the owner(s) on their tax returns.
2. The property is used for a business or income-producing activity, including rental of the property.
3. The property has a "determinable useful life" as defined by the IRS.
4. The property is expected to last more than one year.

## Residential Real Property -- 27.5 years

### Recovery Period

| Month Placed in Service | Year 1 | Years 2-9 | Year 10 | Year 11 | Year 12 | Years 13-27 | Year 28 | Year 29 |
|---|---|---|---|---|---|---|---|---|
| 1 | 3.485% | 3.636% | 3.637% | 3.636% | 3.637% | * | 1.970% | -- |
| 2 | 3.182% | 3.636% | 3.637% | 3.636% | 3.637% | * | 2.273% | -- |
| 3 | 2.879% | 3.636% | 3.637% | 3.636% | 3.637% | * | 2.576% | -- |
| 4 | 2.576% | 3.636% | 3.637% | 3.636% | 3.637% | * | 2.879% | -- |
| 5 | 2.273% | 3.636% | 3.637% | 3.636% | 3.637% | * | 3.182% | -- |
| 6 | 1.970% | 3.636% | 3.637% | 3.636% | 3.637% | * | 3.485% | -- |
| 7 | 1.667% | 3.636% | 3.637% | 3.636% | 3.637% | * | 3.636% | 0.152% |
| 8 | 1.364% | 3.636% | 3.637% | 3.636% | 3.637% | * | 3.636% | 0.455% |
| 9 | 1.061% | 3.636% | 3.637% | 3.636% | 3.637% | * | 3.636% | 0.758% |
| 10 | 0.758% | 3.636% | 3.637% | 3.636% | 3.637% | * | 3.636% | 1.061% |
| 11 | 0.455% | 3.636% | 3.637% | 3.636% | 3.637% | * | 3.636% | 1.364% |
| 12 | 0.152% | 3.636% | 3.637% | 3.636% | 3.637% | * | 3.636% | 1.667% |

* In years 13-27, the rate alternates between 3.636% and 3.637%.

The chart on the preceding page indicates the length of recovery period and the percentage depreciation in each year of ownership of a residential rental property. (Please check with your tax advisor for exact current percentages).

Below is the recovery period table for a non-residential property.

## Nonresidential Real Property -- 39 years

### Recovery Period

| Month Placed in Service | Year 1 | Years 2-39 | Years 40 |
|---|---|---|---|
| 1 | 2.461% | 2.564% | 0.107% |
| 2 | 2.247% | 2.564% | 0.321% |
| 3 | 2.033% | 2.564% | 0.535% |
| 4 | 1.819% | 2.564% | 0.749% |
| 5 | 1.605% | 2.564% | 0.963% |
| 6 | 1.391% | 2.564% | 1.177% |
| 7 | 1.177% | 2.564% | 1.391% |
| 8 | 0.963% | 2.564% | 1.605% |
| 9 | 0.749% | 2.564% | 1.819% |
| 10 | 0.535% | 2.564% | 2.033% |
| 11 | 0.321% | 2.564% | 2.247% |
| 12 | 0.107% | 2.564% | 2.461% |

# Appendix B – 1031 Tax Exchanges

Many savvy investors utilize a powerful tax law that allows the investor to Apass through@ their capital gain to another real estate investment without paying taxes on the gain.  It=s called a 1031 exchange.  It=s a program that allows an investor to sell an investment (such as a rental property, a commercial property, or a business), and use the full proceeds as a down payment on another real estate investment, without paying taxes immediately on the gain.

Although the process is not very complicated, to properly complete an exchange, a buyer should seek the advice of a good accountant and possibly an attorney to assist them in navigating the legal waters of exchanges.  Using an exchange, the Arealized@ gain is not eliminated, but the taxes due are postponed until the client eventually sells the new property.  They may even be able to continue to exchange, thereby Atrading up@ after they've fully depreciated their property, and keep postponing the gain until it passes on to their heirs.

## Avoiding Capital Gains

An investor can defer the taxes that would have been paid on the gain that they made when selling a property.  This gain can be deferred indefinitely.  The investor can even shift money from residential or urban investment properties to commercial real estate.  An investor may, therefore, sell a 4 unit in an urban area and apply all the proceeds to purchase a condo on the beach.

Some investors actually take the equity from a single property and purchase multiple properties with the gain.  For example, let=s say an investor has a 3 unit residential property that they purchased 10 years ago.  Their property is depreciated to the point where the investor would owe a significant percentage of their profit to capital gain taxes.  The investor can sell the building, and use the proceeds to put down payments on 3 investment properties instead of the one they own currently, thereby leveraging their equity.

Exchanges are one method of diversifying or consolidating an investor's portfolio of holdings.  An investor may want to change the type of property in which they=re investing, or an investor may want to use the equity to leverage more property.

## The Ground Rules

**Rule #1**:  For an exchange to work, the property must be sold for a Alike-kind@ property.  Generally, Real Property can be substituted for virtually any other Real Property.  Whether the investor is exchanging a commercial building for a farm, or a multi unit for a shore condo, the new property is seen, in the eyes of the IRS codes, as a continuation of the original investment.

**Rule #2**: The investor cannot ever take possession of the profit or funds from closing. The profit is transferred, at closing, to a certified Exchange Agent. The Exchange Agent then transfers the money to the settlement for the property the investor is purchasing.

**Rule #3**: The third rule is timing. In order to make an exchange work, an investor must identify, in writing, the property which he or she wants to purchase for the exchange, within 45 days of the date he or she sold the original investment property. The investor **can** identify more than one property, just in case one doesn=t work out.

The investor has up to 180 days to complete an exchange, and the IRS does not make extensions. If an investor is exchanging one investment property for two or three, all purchases must be within 180 days of the earliest property sold.

Investors need to avoid taking any boot. Boot is any cash or any other thing of value that is not part of the real estate, like a car or boat received as part of the down payment on the property the investor is selling

# Calculating a Realized Gain for the IRS

When calculating a gain for taxes, you must first determine the Aadjusted basis@ for the property, and then calculate the gain on which you would pay taxes.

**Formula for Adjusted Basis**:

Original Cost: _____

ADD: Improvements: _____

SUBTRACT: Depreciation: _____

EQUAL: Adjusted Basis: _____

**Formula for Realized Gain**:

Sales Price: _____

SUBTRACT: Cost of Sale: _____

SUBTRACT: Adj Basis: _____

EQUALS: Realized Gain _____

# Answer Key

## Chapter 1 Review Questions:

1.   D – Timeshares are a form of Hospitality Property.
2.   True – Classifications are often subjective and can vary from area to area around the country.
3.   B – Building Owners and Managers Association
4.   Office Condominiums or Office Condos
5.   False – Areas in New York and Washington DC have created their own measurement standards.
6.   D – Bathrooms within a unit are considered part of the leaseable square footage.
7.   False – Lifestyle Centers are a form of Open Air Shopping Center.
8.   E – All of the above are open air centers.
9.   False – it is considered a heavy industrial use.
10.  False – Brownfields are redevelopment sites previously used in manufacturing or heavy industrial uses and are generally located in urban centers.
11.  Revenue per available room.
12.  False – Tier two hotels tend to be recently built hotels.
13.  C – Private Residence Clubs are examples of Hospitality Properties.
14.  B – The Sales Price divided by the Gross Income.
15.  B - The Effective Gross Income minus the Operating Expenses.
16.  D – Strengths, Weaknesses, Opportunities and Threats
17.  True.
18.  True.
19.  Earnings before taxes but after deducting reserves.
20.  False.

## Chapter 2 Review Questions:

1.   E – All are common zoning restrictions.
2.   D – The current financing on the building doesn't affect the sales price of the building or property.
3.   D - Vacant Square Footage divided by Gross Leaseable Square Footage
4.   E – All can affect local vacancy rates.
5.   False.
6.   192,000 per year or 16,000 square feet per month.
7.   False – Lifestyle and Colleges can affect business development and companies relocating to an area, which affects demand, which affects property values.

8. Maximum site coverage is (1.2 acres x 43,560 sq ft) x .40 = 20,908.8 sf. The maximum building size is .25 x (1.2 acres x 43,560 sf) = 13,068 sf.
9. 6000 sq ft. (200 per car x 20 cars + a shared back out area of 20x10 x 10 cars)
10. Buried Storage Tanks, Dumping done on property
11. 8.33% (5 vacant months / 60 total months)

## Chapter 3 Review Questions:

1. A – End User
2. True – They hope the appreciation will outweigh the loss
3. Property Flippers
4. B – Tenants in Common
5. B – Scheduled Gross Income
6. $4465
7. C – Owner's Electric
8. False
9. Cap rate = Net Operating Income / Sales Price
10. True
11. C – Internal Rate of Return is not a standard appraisal method
12. True

## Chapter 4 Review Questions:

1. A – Lessor
2. False – in a Gross Lease the landlord pays all expenses
3. Common Area Maintenance Fees
4. D – Triple Net Lease or Net – Net – Net Lease
5. $1979.17 per month (including the CAM fees)
6. False
7. D – Assignment of Lease
8. $4500
9. True
10. Retail Property Leases

## Chapter 5 Review Questions:

1. False.
2. A – Promissory Note
3. $2650.42
4. $336,554.02 (which is $276,554.02 in mortgage + $60,000 down payment)
5. B – Loan to Value Ratio
6. 1.145 ($52,250 per month income / 45,621.84 in interest)

7. Originator
8. Underwriter
9. $219,678.54
10. C – Sub Prime Lender.

**Chapter 7 Review Questions:**

1, True.
2. D – Farming
3. False – within 12 to 18 months.
4. False – Mail to everyone you know.

**Chapter 8 Review Questions:**

1. 1 -Send out a Pre-Listing Package, 2 - Gather Data, 3 - Show up promptly for your appointment, 4 – Smile, 5 - Qualify the Owner's Motivation, Needs and Desires, 6 - Review the Property, 7 - Marketing Presentation, 8 - Handle Questions, 9 - Review Pricing, 10 - Sign the Listing Contracts and required disclosures
2. E – All should be included
3. B – Exclusive Right to Sell
4. C – Open Listing

**Chapter 9 Review Questions:**

1. Loopnet, CoStar, CIMLS, CityFeet
2. Site location, Access Points to Major Highways or Transportation, Zoning Uses
3. Zoning Uses
4. False – Feedback should always be provided to a property owner.
5. False – Staging often helps the buyer tenant to visualize using the property.

**Chapter 10 Review Questions:**

1. Aspects of Buyer Agency include Exercising reasonable professional skill in representation, Having loyalty to client's interests, Treating the client fairly and honestly, Disclosing any potential conflicts, and Advising the client to seek professional advice when the knowledge is beyond the scope of a real estate professional.
2. False – Your client's motivation may not be revealed in negotiations.
3. False – The agent may speak of any properties.

4. False – Our goal is to get the maximum number of clients to reveal themselves to us.
5. False – An agent may always answer questions about other properties.

**Chapter 11 Review Questions:**

1. Property and Building Inspections, Environmental Inspections, Zoning Applications, Zoning Verifications, Review all financial and lease documentation.
2. True.
3. False – Board of Realtor's do not always protect co-broker commissions and particularly do not protect those commissions if the agent or property is not multiple listed.
4. False – Building inspections can include grounds and other structures.
5. C
6. False – Municipalities are different throughout the country. You should always verify any zoning requirements.
7. True.
8. True.
9. E

# Acknowledgements

I'd like to acknowledge and thank the following individuals for their contributions to this text:

**Dr. Michelle Glower** – Professor of Practice at Lehigh University's Goodman Center for Real Estate Studies for her input and review of materials.

**Michael Tubridy** - Global Information Specialist, Albert Sussman Library, International Council of Shopping Centers for his assistance with information on Shopping Center Classifications.

**Betty Broadbent** – Copy Editor for assistance with editing errors, typos and misspellings!

**Theresa Keim** – For putting up with all my crazy ideas!

**Ralph Williams, Dr. Dick McKenna, and Joe Stumpf** - For mentoring at various times during my career.

# For More Information

To subscribe to our ongoing Commercial Real Estate newsletter or to read articles and obtain audio and video training materials by **Loren Keim**, please visit

## **www.RealEstatesNextLevel.com**

# Index